SIFTING THE FEMININE

SERIES EDITOR

Nicole Walker

SERIES ADVISORY BOARD

Steve Fellner

Kiese Laymon

Lia Purpura

Paisley Rekdal

Wendy S. Walters

Elissa Washuta

Sifting the Feminine

Essays on a Woman's Body

ASHLEY ANDERSON

The University of Georgia Press
Athens

Published by the University of Georgia Press
Athens, Georgia 30602
www.ugapress.org
© 2026 by Ashley Anderson
All rights reserved
Designed by Erin Kirk
Set in Arno Pro
Printed and bound by Sheridan Books
The paper in this book meets the guidelines for permanence and
durability of the Committee on Production Guidelines for Book
Longevity of the Council on Library Resources.

Printed in the United States of America
26   27   28   29   30   P   5   4   3   2   1

EU Authorized Representative
Easy Access System Europe—Mustamäe tee 50, 10621 Tallinn,
Estonia, gpsr.requests@easproject.com

Library of Congress Control number: 2025946085
ISBN: 9780820367903 (paperback)
ISBN: 9780820367897 (epub)
ISBN: 9780820367880 (PDF)

IN DEDICATION

To those who have never truly been seen for who they are—

To those who have felt they only existed in the shadows—

To those who have tried and never felt comfortable in the body
their soul lives in—

To those who have lived in worlds not created for you—

To those who have experienced the violence this world has
encouraged against those who are different—

To those who have woken up on a Wednesday . . . or a Monday
or Tuesday or Thursday Friday Saturday Sunday and found themselves
fundamentally less safe than they were the day before—

To those whose lives and identities are always questioned
and criticized and seen as threats—

To those who have lived lives where what is beyond their control
changes how they exist—

To those who have always questioned: the past, the present,
the future, themselves—

To those who have ever dreamed of something different, of the
possibilities—

To those who have looked to the sky, touched the ground, held their lives
and this world in their hands and wondered *why*—

This is yours.

May you feel and be seen and heard and loved and valued for who you are,
appreciated for continuing to exist when that choice is the most difficult one
to continue making with every single breath you take.

And yet—

To those who have chosen fear and hate—

To those who have banned, have outlawed, have supported
legislating how a person exists—

To those who have denied or refused to believe someone
and their experiences—

To those who have told women and girls that they can be anything,
do anything, achieve anything, and then voted against the interests of
those same women and girls—

To those who have, through their actions and words, made the world
less safe for everyone—

To those who have thought that there is only one way to exist—

To those who have told their loved ones they don't matter
through their actions—

To those who have refused to embrace hope and change
and acceptance for everyone—

This is for you, too.

May you learn something about what makes us human.

CONTENTS

ACKNOWLEDGMENTS

The best writing is done when a writer is a part of a supportive and caring community. I am so grateful to have the community of writers who have not only supported me but also the work that this book needed to come to fruition. Thank you to my colleagues and dear friends for the attention, the care, and the support over the years: Hayli Cox, Bailey Boyd, Samantha Edmonds, Ariel Fried, Emily Heiden, Beth Marchbanks, Maurine Pfuhl, Katie Rhodes, Allison Wiltshire, and Suzie Vander Vorste. Your time spent reading drafts, attention while I talked through my ideas, and thoughtful advice, support, friendship, and many cups of coffee have not gone unnoticed or unappreciated.

Community isn't just found in my fellow writers either. To Anna Fox, Briana Bezeredi, Tory Lowe, Brian Stephens, Kanishka Sikligar, and every one of my loved ones who have listened to me talk or laugh or cry about this book, about writing, or about life in general—thank you for being you. I am so fortunate to be surrounded by people who not only support my work but who also support me and all of my chaos as a person.

I also can't go without mentioning my dissertation committee, who supported this project in its previous life before this book was a book. I truly appreciate all of your support, guidance, wisdom, and care over the years. You all have truly helped me become a better writer, scholar, and teacher than I was when I arrived at the University of Missouri; there are not enough words to express my gratitude for everything you have taught me. To Julija Sukys, Becca Hayes, Lynn Itagaki, and Lise Saffran: thank you. Thank you for being the best committee I could have imagined and for being the mentors I needed. You're wonderful.

I would be remiss to mention the editors and publications that gave or are in the process of giving some of the essays in this collection a home. Previous versions of "Locks," "Flash Paper," "Erasing Memory of Skin," and "Field Notes on What Adorns Us: A Case Study" appeared in *Wraparound South* (Winter 2019,) *Hobart* (December 2019), *HAD* (October 2022), *Hive Avenue*

Literary Review (October 2019), and *Quarter After Eight* (2024.) "To Gaze" is forthcoming from *Cosmonauts Avenue*. Thank you to these editors and publications for the time and care they invested in these essays and for giving my work a chance.

Finally, a huge moment of acknowledgment and gratitude to the fine people at the University of Georgia Press, particularly Nicole Walker, Beth Snead, and Sarah Shermyen. Thank you for believing in this project and championing the cause of bringing this book into the world.

SIFTING THE FEMININE

Belly Rubs

Before I get in the shower, I stand in front of the mirror, mostly naked except for an undergarment or two. I look at myself facing the shower, then facing the opposite wall, then head-on. I'm looking for changes that, every morning, are so miniscule I sometimes can't tell they happened. The morning after I've ordered a pizza for dinner or when I'm retaining water, I look at myself from different angles. I sigh. There are mornings when the number on the bathroom scale warns me about the changing shape in the mirror, but there are mornings when it catches me off guard.

The thing I'm looking at in the mirror is my stomach. My belly. Or, as others have referred to it in a disparaging and misunderstood way, my gut. When I hear those descriptions, I flinch. The more space my body takes up, the more the commentary increases in both frequency and severity. Our society has taken the license to say what is on our individual and collective minds and driven off a cliff, one that prioritizes freedom to speak over care, thought, and the consideration that words do damage. Damage that can sometimes be beyond repair.

When my self-esteem and self-image are particularly shaken, I spend longer than I should in the mirror. I examine myself standing with my usual posture. Left angle, right angle, front view. Then the what-if contortions begin. I roll my shoulders back and lift my chest, invoking the proper posture I learned from years of band and choir practice. My chest cavity rises and opens to give my lungs more room and, as a side effect, my stomach takes up less air in front of me. I ask myself as I move space around—what would I look like if there was simply less?

The dissonance of less and more coexisting is not new to me.

I draw in a deep breath of air and hold it in my lungs. My abdominal muscles tighten, and my stomach changes shape. It takes up less space in front of me. My skin wrinkles in reprieve. I exhale and wonder how different my morning routine would be if I didn't have the need to look at myself in the mirror like this. Calculating the amount of time spent scrutinizing my body in the mirror over the course of days weeks months years—lifetimes—instantly weighs on me as a most formidable task even though women are expected to regulate every single cell of their bodies to perfection. In a post-*Roe* world, women are expected to silently accept governments regulating their bodies, too. After all, the need for others to control women's bodies has gone on for centuries.

And yet I do this mirror ritual time and time again, wondering if or when the image in the mirror will ever match the versions of myself—positive or negative—in my head.

※

At a variety of ages, but especially when I was young, other people's comments about my body, particularly how it changed when I was old enough to read and started gaining weight, was enough to send me into tears. I fled to my bedroom and cried it out alone because I didn't want to hear their comments on this way of expressing myself. I knew that those words hurt me, but I couldn't identify that pain until I was well into adulthood because, as a child, I had been taught that pain doesn't exist if you don't see blood along with it.

As I got older, those refrains provoked less of a reaction from me until, somewhere along the transition from my teenage years to adulthood, my response brought about fewer tears and more internal dialogue about people's character. Occasionally, I'd question why they acted this way and those around my peers did not, to my knowledge, say these things about them. Why was I different?

It's a miracle that I'm a writer since, for as long as I can remember, my body shape has been associated with literacy in some way. The connection between something I have a turbulent relationship with, my body, and something that brings me so much joy, reading and writing, doesn't make sense—and yet it does. Maybe it's because I've sought refuge in language because reading and writing don't have to rely on the shape of my body. At times, when I sit down to read or write, I still chastise myself occasionally, letting those intrusive thoughts creep in and ruin a moment of enjoyment. *You'd be so much cuter if it weren't for reading,* those thoughts would say, echoing critiques of the past. *Imagine what you could be if you exercised instead,* as if society has decided that a person can be one or the other, attractive or a reader, but not both.

Worse yet, anyone, not just women, who lives in a body and reads might be exposed to the multitude of ways people exist. They might understand that not all bodies are the same and that is okay. They might rage and rail against lawmakers who spend too much of their time and our resources trying to legislate certain kinds of bodies out of existence or codifying how particular bodies live based on an incredibly and increasingly narrow set of ideas about how the world should work. Reading gives people ideas about themselves and the worlds around them and asks them to think for themselves.

I just want to be—not feel, be—comfortable in my own skin on my own terms.

※

When we talk about silencing and shaming women's bodies, I think of all the times I've gone to a doctor for something wrong with me and the conversation turned from my ailment to my weight. "Well, if you just lost some of the weight, then the problem should resolve itself," they'd say. It didn't matter if the ailment was a persistent cough or my allergies, an aching knee or a routine vaccine. Part of the prescribed cure was the same: lose weight.

On one occasion, I sat on the examining table in a room at my then-university's student health center. I had a skin blemish that had quickly gotten out of control. When I tried to pop it, the spot popped inward and not outward, forcing whatever irritated my skin deeper. The result was a purple lump about three inches long cradling the crook of my neck.

The doctor, an older woman, walked in. If she knew my name or why I was there, it was only based on my paperwork. She never asked questions, not even for my name to make sure she had the correct patient. All I wanted was some antibiotics, some skin care, and to be sent home. No one wants to walk around every day with a purple blob on their neck.

The doctor glanced in my general direction once, twice, as she sat on the stool in front of the computer. "You have to be sick. You can't weigh that much and not be sick."

"But my neck—"

"I'm ordering bloodwork. I'm referring you to an endocrinologist. You need to get this under control. That's probably why you have that lump on your neck," she said, her sentences bleeding together. She paused. "What do you do here?"

"What do I do? I'm a graduate student. I teach English."

"You'll also need a tuberculosis test since you work with children." I protested, saying that I taught at the university—college students—and that I wasn't required to have a TB test on file.

"No, if you teach, you must have a negative TB test on file. That is the law," she said. It wasn't the law.

The doctor took me by the arm and dragged me to the lab, where a technician drew my blood and ran the ordered fasting blood sugar test without question. Blood work like this was not in the original plan. In fact, I had eaten lunch within the last hour. A banana, a bagel with extra cream cheese, and a venti no whip white chocolate mocha, all from the campus Starbucks closest to my office. I'd run out of time to pack a better-for-me lunch that morning. I knew what these results would be—high and inaccurate.

After they took my blood, the doctor handed me a prescription for the antibiotics I wanted to clear up my neck. I hadn't been able to teach, or really go anywhere outside of my apartment, without wearing a scarf for the past week. I had a first date with a guy I really liked in a few days. This lump had to disappear.

"This is for that spot on your neck. I'll call you when I get the results of your blood work in. Come back tomorrow to check the TB test."

The student health center called a few hours later, just as I was about to head into class, to tell me that the results of my tests were in my online patient portal. During the break in my class, I looked at the report. Nothing appeared out of the ordinary.

The next day, I did as I was told and made a trip to campus just to have the TB test read. As the nurse rolled her eyes and listened to my story, the doctor popped her head in. "I have the results of your blood work. Your blood sugar is really high, but everything else looks oddly normal. I've sent the referral to the endocrinologist. Please answer when their office calls you," she said curtly.

The endocrinologist's office called once while I was busy and never called again. Knowing that I would have to walk into yet another doctor's office to be told the same thing, that my body was unruly simply because of its size and that is a problem, didn't motivate me to call back.

⁂

The average human stomach organ is about twelve inches across and measures approximately six inches from top to bottom. The stomach organ, however, can stretch and change shape drastically depending on how much food a person has eaten.

I wonder about my stomach, both the bodily region and the organ itself. Despite its size, my stomach is pretty firm until about my belly button, where firmness quickly transitions into squishiness. After I eat, I can sometimes see what I think is my stomach organ faintly changing the landscape of my skin. Too much food or too much to drink creates a mound that I can feel when I try to smooth it over. If I can put a hand on either side, I feel the change in elevation between the valleys of my palms. Throughout the day, the whole region of my stomach changes shape, not only stretching outward but also gaining in elevation, the slope from my breasts to navel changing from a deflated descent to something looking like the capital letter C.

As a woman, I've been told a countless number of times that my body takes up the wrong kinds of space. My abdomen should swell with the creation of human life that it should be my dream to carry and not grow with food. Breasts and hips can take up some space, but only if they are aesthetically pleasing and full of youth. Things that shouldn't take up space include the rest of my body, my thoughts, my feelings, my sexuality, my achievements, my goals, my anything and everything—because to take up space means I exist and that existence may not always be controlled. To take up space is a certain kind of threat.

⁂

Sometimes, as I read books by women about their bodies, my chest tightens. This time, it's not anxiety or dread that catches my breath in a pause but wonder.

I marvel at their ability to not only process the forms their bodies take, both the ones that help them move through the world and how they translate experiences onto the page. My breath catches when I read these words that describe how bodies are celebrated, are marked, are scorned. But yet, even with the emotions that run through the words and paragraphs I hold in my mind, I find myself pulling my own body closer, unsure if I am ready to release it into this world. I am afraid that, if I share what I have been through, I am also opening myself up to the opportunity to be judged, to be marked, to be scorned more so than I already am. Our society has too much to say about women's bodies, what they should look like. What they should or shouldn't do. Who should make decisions about certain bodies but not others. What words we should use to describe and talk about our bodies and how those words are used. The world is a terrifying place for a body that's different.

After living for so long in a way that the shape of my body has been described to me by other people, often in a way that is cruel and unforgiving and passes judgement on my body and the self that animates it, turning my body into words and encouraging it to dissolve at its edges in a new and different way is a task that tempts terror—because I don't always know what will happen next.

※

The side-by-side pictures of five pounds of muscle and five pounds of fat, reminiscent of the pictures in textbooks for health classes, make me wonder. Just how many inches around my middle are pounds of muscle, and how many are pounds of fat? How important is composition, is shape, is structure, if my first impulse is to critique because it is a part of me?

※

It's not like I haven't tried to make it, my stomach my belly my gut, go away, or at the very least, take up less space. I've tried plenty of interventions, some healthier than others. In junior high, my pediatrician prescribed me Glucophage and then Metformin that were supposed to help me lose weight. Both drugs are typically prescribed to control a person's blood sugar and are usually given to people with diabetes. My pediatrician also sent me to a dietician in seventh and eighth grade, who recommended a low-carb diet. I lost some weight but not enough and not quickly enough to satisfy my doctor. Twenty-five pounds of weight loss a year was the standard, the minimum level of acceptable. It was the goal.

Between marching band and playing sports in high school, I lost more weight, but I didn't make enough progress at the right pace to please anyone.

My doctor upped the dosage from one five hundred milligram pill once a day to one pill twice a day to two pills twice a day. More progress but still not enough.

I started denying myself food the summer between freshman and sophomore years of high school. By the time my senior year came around, I kept feeling faint during marching band rehearsals, even as summer cooled off and turned to fall. "Maybe we should try cutting back on how much she's taking every day," my mom suggested to the nurse at my doctor's office.

The doctor called back and said to cut back to three pills a day, two in the morning and one at night.

When I had a license and a paycheck, I started trying out different weight-loss supplements. I was still not allowing myself to eat what I should but was getting better at acknowledging that my body needed something to keep it alive. I still lost weight but not in the way my doctor or I wanted. I hid the bottles of pills under the clothes in one of my dresser drawers because I was the only one who would look there. First apple cider vinegar pills. Then actual diet pills I didn't have enough discipline to keep up with. To be honest, I don't remember if I even broke the seal on the bottle of diet pills before they expired. Part of me was too scared to open them to begin with.

Why are you doing this? my boyfriend asked.

I had more than enough reasons.

I wanted to be pretty. I wanted to not be a failure. I wanted to be happy. I wanted to be successful. I wanted to not be judged anymore. Stop, take a breath. I wanted to be better.

Better is such a loaded word, I think now, decades later.

But I love you the way you are, he responded.

I wasn't at issue with his love for me. I was up against the lack of love I was taught I should have for the body I found myself in. A body that was unworthy because it didn't conform.

Even now, in my late thirties, I still struggle to admit that I had disordered eating habits as a teenager. I felt and still feel that, if I had made my cries for help more obvious than I did that no one would have taken me seriously until I had become almost nothing. Instead of getting help, I fear I would have been praised for destroying myself.

※

I remind myself that not everything about a stomach, my stomach, is bad or solely worthy of negative critiques. After all, this is the part of me that, if it is warm, keeps me comfortable even when the air outside has chilled.

I remind myself that arms and bodies are what link together in hugs, of the warmth I feel in that moment of embrace. My stomach is the part of me that gurgles, rumbles, expands, and contracts, all the sounds and movements reminding me that I continue to carry on. I have more than one place in the body where a force of life resides.

I remind myself that my stomach, the region, is the center: of gravity, of the body, of the points around which the rest of my physical form takes shape. This is the fulcrum around which I curl myself when I need to compress because the world feels too big. This is the place that allows me to expand, to take up space, to stretch and reach and extend. This is the center that enables the edges of myself to dissolve and reassemble around a core, always finding their way back.

I remind myself.

I remind myself. I remind myself. I remind myself.

❊

I stumble across a conversation on Twitter that, if I hadn't been sitting in my desk chair in my apartment, would have made me do more than just pause.

The thread, tagged #PCOS, was a conversation among women who have the same disease I do, polycystic ovarian syndrome. It's a disease that wreaks havoc on the female body because, when your hormones are out of balance, everything changes: irregular menstrual cycles, changes in hair growth, anxiety, increased risks of diabetes, heart disease, infertility and miscarriages, reproductive cancers—the list goes on and on and on. Because PCOS can be an underlying cause of so many other medical conditions—including disordered eating—the data can only estimate just how many women this disease impacts. One thing it does to me is change the way I look at every part of my body.

And here, on the screen in front of me, women were sharing their stories of how PCOS changed the way their bodies looked. Some women spoke of their bellies, noting that people assumed these women were several months pregnant when, in fact, hormonal shifts, cysts, and bloating made their stomachs take up more space. "If only they knew how many times I've miscarried," one woman added to the end of her post.

Others talk about the struggle of finding clothes that fit and conceal their midsections. Some mentioned that they have the same pairs of pants in multiple sizes so they have clothes to wear as their bodies change shape from day to day. A pair for good days and a pair for bad ones. Those distinctions exist in my wardrobe, too; clothes sorted for good days and bad days. The bad day clothes are stretchy and loose so I don't feel constricted and self-conscious when my body wants to do nothing more than swell and ache. Even when the bad day clothes are too big and no longer fit on the worst of days, I struggle to give them away. *Keep them,* I tell myself. *Just in case.*

I continue to read the thread despite the tightness pulling at the back of my throat. I marvel at the bravery these women have to put their stories on display, to try creating a new narrative out of the ones that other people have imposed on their bodies.

I read about attacks on women's characters. Messy, sloppy. Slovenly. Disrespectful to others, to their spouses, to themselves.

Assumptions about their professional lives, their personal lives, their intelligence—or lack thereof. Misgendering because of their size. Questions about their ability to move through tight spaces.

The comments. The whispers. The stares and glares and sideways glances that come with the territory of taking up space.

I know how they feel. I dread one moment at the beginning of each semester of teaching when I must make a split-second decision as to how I'm going to move about each of my classrooms for the next fifteen weeks.

I know how they feel. Sometimes, it is exhausting to get dressed in the morning, making sure that everything coordinates to show the world that you do, in fact, know how to take care of yourself, of your body that doesn't want to follow someone else's rules.

I know how they feel. I understand what it's like to hear the whispered comments, to see the sideways glances when in the dressing room at a store and you look at yourself in the mirror while wearing something revealing the body underneath the fabric. It makes some people uncomfortable. A well-meaning friend once asked me a question over lunch one time after I told her about another job interview that resulted in a thanks but no thanks follow-up. "Are you sure it isn't the way you look?"

If I had known then what I know now about my body, I probably would have had an answer. I might have said that there are reasons why I look the way I do that I, at the time, did not know about. I might have said that I shouldn't be judged solely on my appearance. I might have said, "I'm trying." Instead, I shrugged my shoulders and picked at my meal.

No matter how visible or invisible my body is, even when in conversation with women who experience the same disease I do, it never gets easier to say that this—this is my body. It isn't perfect and never will be. It doesn't color within the lines.

But it still deserves the same respect as any other body, to receive the same love and acceptance as any other body.

※

When I feel my self-confidence plummeting and my self-image crumbling, my ritual of assessing the shape of my stomach becomes more frequent. I'll take my usual angles before my morning shower. Left side, right side, front view.

I check my reflection in the mirror when it's time to change out of my professional clothes and into whatever outfit I plan to wear next. Sometimes it's workout clothes. Sometimes it's comfy clothes, one of my many T-shirts worn soft by repeated trips through the washing machine and loose-fitting yoga pants. After a long day, it's a tank top and shorts to wear to bed.

I check again. Left. Right. Front. By this point in the day, I've eaten at least two meals and drank more than enough water. There's at least one cup of coffee made almost milky white with creamer. Probably a granola bar rescued from my desk drawer in my office. Most likely some kind of exercise added in, even if that movement was walking around campus. With each angle and the ongoing analysis running in my head, I sigh in exasperation. My stomach is no longer a slope, but something else. On days when I am too much, I feel uncomfortable even in my safest clothes. These are the days where I want to cry but can't always give myself permission. I see the shiny remnants of stretch marks against the paleness of my skin, looking like signs of something trying to claw its way out of me.

Maybe if I let that thing out, that thing that feels so monstrous, then eventually I'll be able to stop. Stop staring at myself in the mirror. Stop . . . what?

I no longer have the willpower to deny myself food. I know when my body starts to protest from a lack of sustenance. My brain becomes the equivalent of a toddler on the cusp of a major tantrum. If I wait too long, the world spins and falls down.

But I still wonder—if I let the monster out, will I feel any better? Will I feel less unruly, less untamed? Will I take up less space?

Maybe the monster is in my head and not my midsection.

Is there a monster to be let out?

Maybe there isn't a monster at all.

Maybe the monster, the monstrosity, isn't trying to claw its way out of me, isn't my body or myself, but is instead what others have told me I should think, feel, or believe about my body. The road to self-acceptance may not mean letting the monster claw its way out, destroying me from the inside, but instead learning to live alongside the monster. Find ways to cohabitate. Create boundaries.

I'm still staring at myself in the mirror. I breathe in using the same techniques that, after all those years of band and choir, have altered the way I take in air. Let the diaphragm do the work. Breathe deeply so that your lungs fill with air and take up space inside of your chest.

If I am aware of my breathing, I see my body change shape. If I hold everything inside—my breath my monsters my pieces of self-image my sense of self-worth—to alter myself, I take up less space and create beauty in a variety of forms. I am constricted, tense. Taught to use the space inside and limit the space outside.

I can only hold my breath for so long.

I feel myself change shape inside and out. This time, the tears pool at the corners of my eyes, threatening to spill over. I can only hold in so much.

I exhale.

Locks

My hair was everywhere. There was always a stray hair resting on the counter in my bathroom, sticking to my clothes, lounging casually on my pillowcase. I found stray hairs stuck in the fibers of my winter coat, in the lint I pulled out of the lint trap in the dryer, or tickling my arm in the middle of the day. Losing a few strands of hair each day is normal and expected for most people. For me, these few strands were here, there, and everywhere.

Finding lost hairs wouldn't have been so much of an issue if my hair didn't pose other problems. My hair was so long that I could no longer wear it down for more than a few minutes before I started to overheat. If I had to be outside with my hair down on a windy day, the breeze blew my hair around so much that the tangles and knots became maddening. Not to mention the amount of shampoo and conditioner it took to keep my hair clean. I hadn't bought or owned a hairdryer in years because, well, what was the point? The effort needed to blow dry my hair wasn't worth it. The frustration was real.

And I'd had enough.

Normally, I would have gone to my usual hairstylist, who runs a small salon a few miles from my parents' house, but she was on vacation for another few days and couldn't fit me in until after I went back to graduate school four and a half hours away. My choices were to continue dealing with the mass of hair growing out of my head or trust a stranger—but at least the salon I found myself at came with a recommendation from my picky sister. The salon appeared to be empty, though, and for a moment, I thought that this was an opportunity for me to back out and casually walk to my car. After all, I hadn't had a haircut in a while—what, three years or so?—and it didn't look bad at all. I didn't need to do this.

Haircuts are complicated for me. Growing up, I never had the chance to tell people what I wanted done with my hair, so I never had control over what my hair looked like. My mom decided to keep it short, creeping around my ears and framing my face in a way that made me look too soft and pudgy. As a kid, I thought I looked too much like a boy—chubby stature, short hair, refused to wear dresses—before I understood why my mom kept such a tight rein on my hair. It was chaotic. I couldn't braid my hair like the rest of my fellow Brownies for World Friendship Night for Girl Scouts or wear the sideways ponytails that were the rage in elementary school. My hair always looked like something not my own, a fluffy mop plopped on my head. By the time I was old enough to have control over the top of my head, I felt inept to figure out what to do with it.

Hell, I still don't know what to do with it, which may be why I usually try to avoid haircuts. I don't know the angles and layers and shapes. I don't have the vocabulary to make sense of my hair.

When the hairstylist asked me how much I wanted to cut off, I froze again. Her blond curls stood out in stark contrast against my dark brown ones in the mirror. I am not a numbers person, instead choosing to specialize in words and phrases instead of numerals and measurements. Six inches didn't feel like enough, but a foot felt like too much of a commitment. "Where would nine inches hit?"

The hairstylist rubbed the side of her hand against the middle of my upper arm. Considering I could almost sit on the ends of my hair, nine inches was a drastic change that, because of the thickness of my hair, had to take place one small snip at a time. Giving my hair one solid cut would most definitely break the stylist's shears. My heart rate picked up and I tried to hide the fact that I couldn't catch my breath. Was nine inches too much, too fast? I watched as the hairstylist got out her shears and prepared to cut my hair. Was that enough to get rid of what I was tired of carrying around?

As I nodded, saying nine inches was a good length to cut, I raced through the possible outcomes in my head.

My heart sped up, and I wondered what the heart rate monitor in my Fitbit registered at that moment. I felt myself sweating but couldn't decide if it was from having my blanket of hair covering my back or if it was the anticipation of those first few snips.

The hairstylist picked up her shears, and I closed my eyes as she stepped behind the chair. *Stay calm,* I told myself. *Just keep breathing. It will be okay in the end.* The faint sound of sharpened metal against dead protein sounded like a cheese grater against my nerves as the woman cut the first locks of hair from my head, snip by snip.

One inch

My tiny rural northeast Ohio hometown has six churches within the township limits. Each church dictated how my friends and I grew up. The two Baptist churches and the Methodist church invited only the Boy Scouts to a special Scout Sunday service twice a year. The Congregational Church hosted a pancake breakfast each year after the Memorial Day parade, the one and only parade my hometown hosted. Nearby, there was yet another church, the Catholic Church with its own grade school. Church events sometimes determined who could or would go to middle school and high school dances. For those whose parents insisted that the whole family be in the pews on Sunday morning, church swayed plans for sleepovers and birthday parties, the start time of Sunday sporting events, and whether a carwash fundraiser should start midmorning or midafternoon.

The church that intrigued me the most, however, was further from the beaten path than the others, both literally and ideologically. Unlike other churches, the Apostolic Pentecostal was not located on either of the town's main roads. It seemed as if it had been dropped from the clouds onto a plot of land surrounded by duplexes and a bunch of trees. The fact that the parking lot was full on both Wednesday and Sunday nights wasn't what piqued my curiosity. It was the fact that I only knew four people who went to that church.

One of the few times any of the kids, a pair of sisters and a brother-sister pair, talked about church was when, on the school bus, someone asked one of the girls about her hair. She was a grade behind me and sassy to the point of mean. "Why is your hair so long?" someone asked. Most of the girls I grew up with had varying lengths of long hair, but I did not. As a child, hairstyles were something that I associated with age: little girls had long hair, moms had hair somewhere in the middle, and grandmas had short hair. That was all I saw in the world around me, women who cut their hair shorter as they aged.

"Because I'm not supposed to cut my hair. If I do, I'll get in trouble at church," she said, flipping her waist-length plait of perm perfect curls back over her shoulder. She sensed our confusion. "We learned in church that girls aren't supposed to cut our hair because it's what makes us special."

I still didn't get it. My mom and my PBS cartoons told me that I was special for other reasons: my sense of humor, my willingness to help other people, my talents, my hobbies, etc., but not because of my hair. As I got older, I learned that, in certain denominations of Christianity, women are discouraged from cutting their hair. In the Apostolic Pentecostal Church, women do not cut their hair because it is believed that a woman's hair is a holy cover, an interpretation of a verse from 1 Corinthians 11. This passage, verses one through sixteen, describes a woman's long hair as being a source of her glory. Women who do not have their heads covered during prayer or prophecy bring dishonor to themselves. Within a woman's hair lies power apparently. The power to prove she is worthy of . . . something. Attention? Acceptance? Love? Womanhood?

Or is it a woman's hair that takes her power away?

Years and years later, while I worked on this essay, a college friend said, "Do some research on the context of that verse." As someone who is perpetually curious, I did some reading. There are several variations of how these verses are interpreted, even among biblical scholars, and especially outside of evangelical groups. Most likely, Paul wasn't telling people not to cut their hair but instead was asking the Corinthians to think about the meaning of their hair in two cultural contexts that existed within the city. There's more at stake than just hair. Tolerance. Acceptance. Coexistence. Community.

Later that day, the day when the question of cutting hair came up at school, I asked my mom why the girls who went to the church down the road weren't allowed to cut their hair. "Well, some people think that's what's best for them and God," she said.

"Then why do I get my hair cut all the time?"

"Because until you learn to take care of it yourself," my mom said, "I will tell you what to do with your hair."

Two inches

My mom has a collection of stories about my childhood that she likes to tell. One of these stories spans a couple of decades, implicating my grandmother and Shirley Temple.

Grandma McKnight, my mom's mother, kept an autographed picture of Shirley Temple on the mantle in the formal living room. The photograph was a fixture in Grandma's house; I never remember it not being on the mantle because it had sat there, in its frame, for decades. Grandma told me the story of the one time she met Shirley Temple when they were children— my grandma and Shirley Temple were only eight months apart in age—at a launch of Shirley Temple-inspired dresses at the local Woolworth's in Grandma's hometown of Johnstown, Pennsylvania. I listened because Shirley Temple's place in my childhood spanned beyond one close encounter with Grandma over half a century before I was born. As a toddler, my dark brown hair grew in perfect spiral curls that bounced and twirled around pockets of air. My mom told me how I received compliments on my hair before I was old enough to know what a compliment was. At two years old, I even got confused for a baby-sized version of Shirley Temple in the stuffed animal aisle of our local K-Mart. "Mom, this lady has a baby Shirley Temple in her cart!" a young girl screamed as my mom and I searched for a new toy. I was unfazed by what happened.

The comparison didn't just stop with a couple of chance encounters. Because of my hair, my family got into a habit of buying me Shirley Temple movies as gifts. I willingly watched and helped put the VHS tapes of remastered movies into the VCR. I took my place somewhere in the living room—the middle of the floor or, as I got older, on the couch or taking the movies upstairs to my bedroom—and watched. Despite seeing the pictures of me as a toddler, I wondered why my family continued to add to this collection as I got older, a gathering of videotapes in plastic cases that took up an entire shelf of the video rack in the coat closet. I didn't see the comparison, especially after my hair ceased to look like hers.

Decades later, while Grandma spent her declining years at her home next door, someone snuck the original copy of Shirley Temple's autograph out of the house and replaced it with a copy in the same frame. Grandma's mind was falling down around her, and my aunt, Grandma's caretaker, kept shuttling Grandma's possessions out as quickly as possible, convinced that Grandma was days or weeks away from death's door. "I just wanted to make sure you have this," someone said, handing me the original eight-by-ten-inch headshot in a frame we found in one of the upstairs bedrooms at Grandma's house. I took it and hung it on my bedroom wall, then the living room wall of my first apartment. Each time I took the picture down to move somewhere else, it tore pieces of paint and plaster off the wall. Maybe Shirley was trying to say something after all these years, her message hidden just below a surface I never bothered to graze before. Maybe there was more to Shirley Temple's story, and even to my own story, than just pretty curls on the heads of smiling little girls.

Three inches

Four inches

Five inches

I was in fifth grade when I convinced my mom to let me grow my hair out. In retrospect, I probably wasn't mature enough to handle the responsibilities of having long hair. While my classmates experimented with their mothers' makeup, I ran around the yard making up stories of jungles and pioneers in my head. While my classmates played with curling irons, I continued to find more and more ways to avoid taking care of my hair. But I wanted to pin the butterfly clips in my hair and pull it through the ponytails and brightly colored scrunchies that my peers did, so I finally convinced my mom to let me grow it out. When she said yes, I felt more like an adult. I had responsibilities now beyond loading the dishwasher every other night and keeping my bedroom clean.

"Oh Lord, are you in for it," Nancy, my Girl Scout troop leader and one of the few local hairstylists, said at my last regularly scheduled haircut. Nancy herself was a fiercely opinionated redhead who smoked too much and rubbed too many adults the wrong way.

At first, I thought having this responsibility and growing hair was great. No more haircuts every six weeks. No more fighting over the background color of my school pictures every fall. As my hair got to an awkward length, though, I came to understand just how much responsibility came with having hair like my friends.

This realization came to a head when my mom, one day in the early summer between fifth and sixth grade, tried to brush a rat's nest out of my hair. With each pluck of a comb or a hair pick, I felt my scalp's nerve endings snap to attention. I grew tired of having to deal with the rhythmic yanks pulling the skin of my head away from the tissue beneath. "Stop!" I cried. "It hurts!"

"Well, if you'd take better care of your hair, then it wouldn't hurt so bad!" my mom replied.

More yanks. More tears. More exclamations from someone—me—who quickly realized that being a tomboy, or for that matter being a young woman, hurt more than I wanted it to. "Stop! You're hurting my head!" I yelled at my mom. I never yell at my mom, who is a quiet and gentle soul. She is the kind of mother who would sigh and remind me in a calm tone that *this is what happens when you don't take care of something,* as if this encounter with my hair and a hairbrush were on the same level as an injury to a well-loved toy or a tear in a favorite piece of clothing. She was the one who was always ready with cookies for a Girl Scout meeting and would take a day off work to help chaperone a field trip to the zoo. Today, for some reason, was different. Maybe it was my mom being a person with limits to her frustration. Maybe it was the early summer heat in our house that didn't have air conditioning.

I got up and stormed out of the living room. I passed the stairs and rounded the corner to the entry hallway where I came face to face with my dad, a large, surly figure whose presence intimidated almost everyone who crossed his path. My dad worked a lot of long hours in a loud and noisy plant that cut and processed structural steel. This was probably his only day off that week, and in the hours on his days off and in the evenings, his requests for quiet—except for the sound that he made—were one slight step away from demands. When my friends came over to play, they described my dad as scary and mean. He took a step closer, and by reading the expression on his face, I knew that I had crossed a line.

There are times when I allow myself to remember what happens next, but there are just as many, if not more, times where I have made so many excuses for why the scene played out the way it did. I've become ambivalent and unable to see the situation for what it is and what it could be. More often than not—both in the moment and decades later—I try to play it off as if nothing happened, as if this moment didn't somehow break a piece of me that has yet to be glued back together.

Something did happen, though. I felt so many things that the logical first response was to cry because processing what had happened, at the time, was a lot for an eleven-year-old to deal with. I was frustrated because I just wanted my hair left alone. I was angry because my mom didn't understand just how much it hurt to have my hair brushed that way. I was scared because of my dad.

I still think about the consequences of this moment today. The way I don't like to be in tight spaces. The way the sounds of slamming doors or heavy footfalls make me tense up. The most dependable way to make me cry is to have someone raise their voice with the slightest hint of anger. I react with tears despite hearing that raised, angry voice for as long as I can remember, probably for my entire life. I don't like having people I don't trust in my personal space when I sense it is difficult to quickly escape. Crowded elevators, restaurants with tables and chairs too close to one another, even middle seats—they all make my heart speed up if I can anticipate an unknown person's skin touching mine. More often than not, even the thought of contact makes me tense up. It was then, in that confrontation with my dad, that I first realized there was something dangerous about my hair.

Suddenly, long hair didn't seem worth it anymore, but I still let it grow.

My hair grew. And grew. And grew. It grew so long that it changed colors, and when my mom took me in for a haircut before my freshman year of high school, she asked why the last few inches of my hair were the color of straw. "It's because the ends are dead," Nancy said during one of the last haircuts she gave me before she moved away. "That's what happens when your hair grows too fast."

I wonder if that is what happens when a person's hair grows too fast, or if it's the outward result of idealism dying on the inside too quickly.

Six inches

Seven inches

Eight inches

Earlier that November evening, just two months before my thirtieth birthday, I spent a considerable amount of time in front of my bedroom mirror, trying to figure out what to do with my hair. Style, shake head in disgust, start over. I wanted my hair away from my face but still soft enough that I felt pretty. Wanted, maybe. It had been so long since I had been on a date that my nerves had gotten the best of me.

A few hours later, I stood on my tiptoes in the entryway of his house, white walls and light hardwood floors flanking a white door that only locked with a little convincing. He, a burly man with a mess of almost black hair and beard, pulled me closer. He had at least a foot on me in terms of height, so to think about getting close enough to kiss him, I had to stand on my tiptoes. He had his fingers wound through my hair, giving my locks a gentle tug. "I didn't take you for someone who would like this," he said, pulling away slightly. I probably wasn't supposed to like this, being treated a little on the rough side by a man who I hadn't known for very long at all. To be honest, I don't know when I was or wasn't told how I should or should not like to be touched in this kind of situation beyond talk about consent. In any other context, having anyone pull my hair would cross boundaries of safety and respect, but this was somehow . . . different. Instead, I wondered how much longer we were going to linger at the door.

"I guess I'm just full of surprises," I responded, my voice registering from somewhere deeper in my throat.

It was true. I surprised myself with how quickly I let myself get close to this man. After our first date just a week or so before that night we kissed long and passionately by his front door, I agreed to go back to his house after dinner at a local restaurant with a view of the city of Cincinnati that made me wonder why I would ever want to live anywhere else. Originally, we intended to just watch a movie and talk somewhere quieter than the restaurant. My friends, who wanted the details of my first date since a messy but quiet breakup with my high school sweetheart over Labor Day weekend, kept sending me text messages. While they asked if they needed to send a search party, fearing that the reason I wasn't responding to their messages was because I had gone on a date with a psycho axe murderer, I was falling into bed with this man after our first date, something I hadn't done before. Ever.

"Wow. You're so beautiful," he whispered as he slowly ran his slightly calloused hands over first my ribs, then my side, then my hip. I tried not to blush, and as he pulled me closer to him in the middle of his king-sized bed, I briefly wondered what was so wrong with what we were about to do in the first place. Deep down, I knew that this was my body's response to the first earnest touch from a man who desired me in years. My ex and I spent the last couple of years of our relationship avoiding intimacy of almost any kind.

But at this moment, here and now, at age twenty-nine, I wanted to know that my body still had the power to be desirable because in a lot of ways I didn't feel like I could be wanted after such a long time of being pushed away.

Back by the door after our second date, he further knotted his fingers in my hair, tugging with a little more earnest. "Indeed," he said to my response about being full of surprises. I wondered just what I was getting myself into as I remembered what desire felt like.

Nine inches

I see the dark hair creeping all over me, slowly making its way out of not-quite-alabaster skin and covering places that, according to society, should appear hairless on a woman's body. My stomach. My chest. My face.

I know why that hair is here, emerging from my skin no matter what I do to remove it and vainly attempt to maintain a "normal" feminine appearance, or at least what we've been taught to understand as womanly. It's because something is happening inside my body, manipulating my hormones and forcing me to watch my diet, exercise more and sit less, and take birth control pills every day without fail. A diagnosis caught years after it should have been, hoping that the disease stays manageable while the hair, one of the many outward symbols of what is going awry inside of me, destroys me even more.

"Why is this happening to me?" I asked time after time. Rhythms not established. Odd hairs growing in places they shouldn't be. Missed cycles. Fear and uncertainty that I would never know what was happening to my body.

"Why is this happening to me?" I asked when, during the summer of my twenty-ninth year, my body revolted against me for almost three weeks out of every six. After years of seeing nutritionists, trying low carb diets and portion control, and following every set of instructions my previous doctors gave me, nothing worked.

You are not normal, the tracking app where I logged my cycle and how I felt each day kept saying but not saying. The repeated alerts with "that's odd," or the number of days I felt this way in the past month created a subtext further reinforcing that something was wrong.

I see what the same disease has done to my friends, the pills and injections and diabetes diagnoses, the sleep apnea and the weight issues and the chronic fatigue syndrome, the funerals for babies born too soon. But when those four letters—PCOS, or polycystic ovarian syndrome—come up in conversation after another friend is labeled, the same line comes up in response from someone who has been there, too—"Well, at least you didn't get the facial hair like some women do."

But I did, and as I watch the Facebook videos and screenshots of Instagram posts of women who said *screw it* to the razors and waxing and other hair removal methods to make them look like nothing is wrong with the chemicals pulsing through their veins, I wish I could be so brave. Instead, I shave it off as often as I can. Hide it. After all, it was the same Gillette brand as what I have in my shower that told women to shave off their body hair as early as 1915, the year the first razor for women was released to the public. It was important, though, not to call the act of women removing hair *shaving* because the term was decidedly too masculine, according to the Smithsonian. Just as the companies who made razors would soon send them to soldiers off at war, there was also a fight about language, about how to describe the same practice performed by different people.

Gillette wasn't the only one, but instead a moment in a long line of products that slowly, methodically, waged war on women's hair. Historians note that first, advertisements for depilatories and waxes and potions came after the hair on women's faces and arms. Then, as fashion trends changed and the American fixation on cleanliness grew with the onset of the Roaring Twenties, advertisements in magazines such as *Harper's Bazaar* and *McCall's* called for the removal of underarm hair, citing new fashionable dresses with sheer sleeves, or no sleeves at all, and the bacteria that underarm hair could harbor. In 1930, an article in *Hygeia* described removing arm, underarm, and leg hair as a social convention. By 1964, 98 percent of women ages fifteen through forty-four removed body hair.

These attitudes about hair aren't the case everywhere. Sikhism forbids any form of hair removal regardless of one's gender. The Bahá'í Faith doesn't have as hard and fast rules about hair removal but discourages the practice unless someone is removing their hair for medical reasons. Some Hindu and Buddhist groups shave the heads of children. The particularly American emphasis on where hair should and should not be, especially for women, is not isolated nor universal.

It makes me feel odd, scared even, my hair. Scared of what my hair means. What the presence of my hair where it "should" and "should not" be has the potential for as meaning expands outward.

In some ways, it makes me feel out of control. Powerless.

I am baffled by the power that comes with hair. In one moment, I feel the weight of it upon my head, blowing in the breeze and capturing the attention of the world to assert that yes, this is where I'm told my glory supposedly resides, but I don't feel glorious. I wonder what I did to make some celestial being both bless and curse me at the same time, to have this stuff growing out of my head that makes me supposedly wanted and desired but also crawling across my skin, making me feel repulsive. I fear undressing in front of my mirror in my bedroom because, beneath the multiple layers I wear to keep my midsection covered, the fine but wiry black hair creeps across my stomach, the ends reaching for each other to close me in.

Instead, I feel like a beast in my dark follicle-framed cage, a century-old circus attraction who missed the memo that the show was over, a body who is human and yet not at the same time. In light of the low carb diet, the 150 minutes of exercise a week, and the take your pills reminder—birth control for hormones, iron for anemia, B12 to help iron absorption, magnesium for the migraines—and the hope-for-the-best kind of lifestyle I find myself in, the growth that inches across my skin makes me feel powerless as to what my body is doing to itself. Despite my best attempts, I am unwillingly destroying myself from the inside, with my only cry for help being the unruly hair covering my body that I don't want others to notice.

※

"What do you think?" the hairstylist asked as she brushed my hair in different directions, making sure that everything was the same length.

What did I think? A lot went through my head at that moment. As I looked at myself in the mirror, I started calming down. The haircut didn't look nearly as bad as my terror led me to imagine. There was a noticeable difference in my hair, but not so much that my jawline and cheekbones melded into that shapeless blob of flesh I feared. I was still me, just with a little less of the hair I had a complicated relationship with.

There was more to this haircut than simply snipping strands and shaping the mass growing out the top of my head. I had attempted to take back control of one uncontrollable part of my body, to make some effort at reclaiming my sense of womanhood, even if that womanhood looks different. At an age when I had thought I had come into my own as a person, I was still learning to live as a person with an illness, but not one that people held fundraisers for or sponsored awareness months or ran 5Ks for to find a cure.

Sometimes, I wonder if it would be easier if my illness left me without hair. Instead of the course black strands growing in places where hair wasn't supposed to be recognizable, I wonder if it would make it easier to explain my disease if I walked through this world with a scarf tied around my head to hide my baldness. Or, if I had the courage, to simply move through this world with a bare head, challenging the notion that I, as a woman, needed to have a head full of glowing hair to be what I say I am.

But no one is going to make a PCOS awareness T-shirt to wear. There are no fights against this disease like there are obesity and cancer and diabetes, although all three of those conditions can be associated with the disease I have. There are no rallies, no color-themed sporting events. The merchandise displays don't appear in stores but instead find a home on the internet. No one cares about the ovaries that don't work properly or the wanton hair growing on bodies because it's hard to sexualize a disease when you can't see the parts that aren't functioning properly. Or when the disease transforms a body into something that we, as a society, have determined is part woman and part . . . something else.

The only fight here is against my hair.

It is something I sit with in an uneasy silence of acceptance, knowing that I am not alone but also knowing that most of the outside world will not see or hear about the kind of body I inhabit. The kind of hair I have to cut, shave, disguise. Live with, deal with. Try to make those closest to me understand and, hopefully, accept as well.

Even with acceptance, though, comes some degree of pain. Not everyone understands just what chronic fatigue does to you by the time Friday evening rolls around and the thought of going out with friends or colleagues seems impossible because you have used all your energy for the day. The pain of having to tell someone you love that trying to have a family of more than just two may be the most difficult thing you as a couple will ever have to face.

I ran my fingers through my newly cut hair, feeling the stubble by my ear graze the back of my hand ever so slightly. For the first time since my diagnosis, I had a say in what my hair looked like, what it did, where it went. In this tensely fleeting moment, I felt beautiful again.

That moment and my silent acceptance didn't last long. A few short weeks after this haircut, millions of women would take to the streets on my thirtieth birthday to protest the incoming president's policies against women and to assert that women of all types have voices and rights, too. Continued efforts to strip me and millions of other women who relied on birth control not only to avoid pregnancy but to also simply function on a daily basis resulted in women dressing up as Offred from Margaret Atwood's novel *The Handmaid's Tale*, marching and protesting decisions made to police women's bodies. If I were a creation of Atwood's imagination that, for many women, wasn't imaginative but a reflection of hundreds of years of oppression, I would have been sent south to The Colonies to clean up radiation, my skin peeling off until I died.

An unwoman, as they called us in the book.

Little did we know how far these policies would go.

My acceptance of my disease was no longer silent, my body no longer quiet, my hair no longer something that was just there but instead, by virtue of being a part of my body, became a site of political debates so loud that you couldn't help but hear them screaming. Before I knew it, I found myself writing to my lawmakers telling them just what it took for me to function on a daily basis, why I needed affordable access to quality health care, and why those seemingly tiny twenty-eight-packs of beige and brown pills had such a huge impact on my ability to live, work, and enjoy life in a way that felt something like normal. I had a way to feel something like me. I felt the impending doom lingering on the horizon, the possibilities of what would happen if people who didn't understand got their way.

Unruly hair, covering me even more quickly. My stomach. My chest. My face. The reality of living in a world where I had fewer rights than my mother did at my age closing in like the bars on a cage to contain the monster that I am simply because I am a woman. In the coming years, my hair would become the least of my worries.

It won't get easier, telling people about my disease. *But your story needs to be out in the world*, my activist friends tell me. *You're so brave*, they add. But I never feel brave. I feel the desperation in my voice each time I email and fill in comment boxes on petitions—*Please don't take this away from me*.

What *did* I think of my haircut?

My pulse slowed as I let out a long-held sigh of relief that I kept buried in my lungs for most of the time I sat in the chair. This was my hair—not a disease's hair, mine. I had a say in how it was displayed in this world.

"I like it," I said as a smile grew across my face.

Looking back, I don't know if I can say I feel the same way anymore.

Flash Paper

No one ever came out and said it, but I always got the idea that I was supposed to be seen and not heard.

"You're being too loud!"

"Can't you stop talking?"

"Quiet!"

My mother never tried to silence our voices, the voices of my sisters and me. *It's because your dad hears noise at work all day*, the adults said. *He just needs some quiet.*

❋

Used in the world of special effects, flash paper burns instantly, not leaving behind smoke or ashes. Once ignited, flash paper only exists for a brief moment before it ceases to be. Flash paper remains only as a memory.

❋

I started talking late, so late that my mother, who sat in her rocking chair while her pregnant body glided back and forth, back and forth while reading all the late 1980s' books on how to raise a child, took me to the family doctor when I hadn't started talking on time. As a first-time parent, she was worried that there might be something wrong with me.

Dr. Castaldi, our family's primary care doctor, checked me over from head to toe, in my eyes and mouth and ears, and issued his diagnosis. "There's nothing wrong with her," he said, reassuring my mom. "She just doesn't have anything to say yet."

※

It is easy to make flash paper. One will find various instructions on the internet, as well as cautions against mixing strong acids without the proper safety gear. One website says that their instructions will leave you with "professional-grade material you can use to astonish your family and friends!"

I wonder if there are more dangers in the creation of flash paper than the mixing of strong acids without safety equipment. Combining multiple strong compounds into one space poses a risk, especially in a space that is purposefully fragile. One may not know what that purpose is, but fragility works in ways that are both incredibly beautiful and dangerous.

※

My favorite and only story of childhood rebellion usually involves learning how to speak properly.

In third grade, my school assigned me to speech therapy because I allegedly spoke with a slight lisp. "Snake, sit, sand, spell," the speech therapist said, exaggerating the ways in which her mouth made "s" sounds properly.

I saw nothing wrong with the way I spoke. In fact, I was angry and upset that I was the only one of my friends, a group that largely consisted of kids who were labeled as talented and gifted, to be pulled out of art class every other week to sit in the scary, windowless therapy room in the basement of our century-old primary school. "Thnake, thit, thand, thpell," I repeated back.

"I'm sorry, but there's nothing we can do for your daughter," the speech therapist told my mom at parent-teacher conferences. "She just won't cooperate."

"That's because there's nothing wrong with her in the first place," my mom said.

Eventually, my speech sorted itself out, not for the work of a speech therapist, but by way of me growing into the sounds I needed.

※

The key to making flash paper work is nitric acid. The more scientific name for flash paper is nitrocellulose, a combination of nitric acid and cellulose (paper). Nitrocellulose sounds far less exciting and awe-inspiring than flash paper, but as with many scientific names, the purpose here is not to incite awe and wonder at the world around us but instead describe and categorize based on composition and function.

Nitric acid is created by mixing distilled nitrates with sulfuric acid. The resulting mixture is colorless or pale yellow in color. The acid does not occur naturally and is only made in laboratories but, once mixed, has corrosive qualities and is said to react violently with materials not made of metal.

Nitric acid is not the only scientific creation that reacts violently against established categories and distinctions with which it does not wholly agree.

※

I've never been good at talking about my feelings. Whatever the root cause is—fear, insecurity, my knack at internalizing all the bad parts of the world and making them my fault—makes me freeze when someone asks me how I'm feeling. "Oh, I'm fine," is my default frozen response. When I thaw, the response begins as a trickle and slowly builds to a flood.

As a teenager, I took my feelings out on my body as a way of coping with them. My feelings were objects I needed to put away, and my body seemed to be the perfect and only place I could put those emotions. Now, the physical scars are so faded that they are barely noticeable, but the memory is still there. Sometimes, I feel the invisible hands of my frustrations grabbing my arms and shaking me. The urge to use my body as a place of destruction hasn't welled up in years, but those arms and hands of frustration and anger still find their way to me.

I hear the voice of a memory inside my head. I drift back to the only time I allowed the blades of my razor to sing across the skin of my stomach in the shower, speaking words that I could not say out loud. The boyfriend, both of us in high school, seeing the two thin scratches the next time we fooled around, stopped. "Please don't," he said, pulling me closer to him as everything came to a halt.

I wonder why it is his voice that speaks my memory instead of my own.

※

To make flash paper, one must first set up a well-ventilated workspace. Put on protective clothing: gloves, apron, goggles. Carefully mix nitric acid, sulfuric acid, and baking soda. Use 100 percent pure cotton paper. Soak the paper in acid. Soak the paper repeatedly in water to wash away excess acid. Another series of soakings and dryings that must always be maintained at a distance from the human experience that flash paper aims to create.

The most important step is that the creating must happen underneath the ventilation hood, but the creator must not be under the hood. The maker must be separate from the experience.

⁂

In graduate school, when I first discovered and read French feminist theory, a lot of aspects about the way people communicate suddenly made sense. The idea that language is patriarchal and women's experiences are unrepresentable by language systems clicked in my head. The silence of women suddenly became loud with my newfound exposure to the theory behind what I had internalized all along but didn't have a name to put to the idea.

The more I read, the more my voice's experience made sense. Women's voices. The ways in which mine always seemed to stand out, too loud, against the quiet whispers of those around me.

Be quiet.

You're too loud.

Stop talking.

You make a lot of noise.

Irigaray, Cixous, Kristeva.

The longer I sat with these theorists and thought about them, I wondered if it isn't so much that women's experiences are unable to be represented by language. I wonder if there's a disconnect between describing experience and comprehending experience. Maybe there was a time and place where this disconnect did not exist—maybe—but maybe we have gotten to a point where there are words to describe women's experiences. Maybe that language does exist. The problem is in others understanding and comprehending those words and the experiences they represent.

You need to learn to control your volume.

You sure do have a set of lungs.

If I can hear you, you're too loud.

Quiet down!

The realization that my voice was never meant to be heard both devastated and motivated me. As the world suddenly shifted and those in charge of

Washington silenced more and more women's voices, I found myself speaking louder and louder.

❀

To ignite a piece of flash paper, do the following:
1. The flash paper to a neutral location.
2. Hold the flash paper with something other than your hands. A pair of tongs or forceps are recommended, although the cartoon hand in the picture looks like it's using tweezers.
3. Light a match.

The key to experiencing flash paper is distance. The creator cannot be included in the experience.

❀

The number one way to set me on fire is to tell me to be quiet because I don't know what I'm talking about when, in fact, I do. In the moments that it takes the fire to ignite, I become guilty of intellectual snobbery and remind myself of all the years I've spent in school. I remind myself of the experiences I've had in my thirty-some years of life that I never told others about because I've decided there are parts of my life I don't want them to know. Language deeming my experiences unrepresentable.

❀

There is a dangerous side to flash paper, though. When combining multiple volatile compounds into a small space, there is always the chance that something will go wrong without attention and care. Toxic compounds can form. The creator can inhale those fumes and experience damage to their lungs, their brains, their bodies. The risk of damage to others increases.

It's almost as if flash paper were a metaphor for speech, that without attention and care, damage will be done. People will lose their rights. People will not be able to access the care and resources, the tools and the education, the places and voices that enable them to live authentic lives as people who are happy and healthy and heard. *See me! Hear me! Acknowledge me! Protect me! Help me!* the voices of people at the margins say. *Show us the lives we want are possible!* they shout. *Where is the magic?*

Too many creators of flash paper do not pay attention, do not treat others with care, do not acknowledge that they have done damage and continue to break and smash and destroy the lives the creators claim to respect and value. *I know better!* they say as they dismantle the hoods and dispose of the gloves and ignore the safety precautions. *You have nothing to worry about!* they scream as the mechanisms to protect us falter, stumble, crumble, and disintegrate into nothing more than a memory of how our mothers had more rights than we do.

Everything feels so much bigger and yet the walls move in closer and closer as we shout and scream; yet the creators have invested in only one precaution to keep them safe—earmuffs.

❋

Those moments I've kept from others come to mind when I wonder if they heard or understood what I had to say. They pile up on one another. This is where I wonder if the theories surrounding language and representation and women's experiences have evolved over time, or if maybe they could use some expansion. As I get older, I oscillate between thinking about these moments as language not being able to describe my experiences and the inability or unwillingness of listeners to comprehend.

Each time the silence and the accompanying realization washes over me, it happens again.

A few clicks of anticipation.

The first lick of flame on the paper.

The flash!

The awe of the crowd, except in my mind, half the crowd is speaking and wonders why they aren't being heard.

I wonder—what do we miss out on in those moments of anticipation and awe because we only hear part of the message?

Smile!

"Smile, Ashley! Why you gotta look so serious?"

❄

Most people know me because of my facial expressions. By nature, I am an animated communicator, and, apparently, the filter for nonverbal communication never quite developed. Sometimes, my face says what my mind holds back. Mostly, though, I am known for almost always having a face that reflects pleasantness, warmth. My face says that I am a person who is approachable and friendly.

When I was in middle and high school, my friends would challenge me to make a mean or angry face while we rode the school bus up and down the back country roads. I contorted my face into what I thought was something mean or angry: scrunched eyebrows, lowered chin, narrowed eyes. After a minute or two, someone called off the challenge with laughter. "I don't think Ashley is capable of making a mean face," a classmate said.

"I don't think I am either," I said as the school bus hit another pothole or bump in the road.

❄

"Smile, Ashley! You look like an old sourpuss!"

❄

According to an article in the *International Journal of Psychology*, social perception studies show that people who smile are viewed more favorably than those who don't smile and that this perception is more commonly held by women than men. Women are also more positive in how they interpret other people's smiles, with women finding people who smile to be more trustworthy. This same article reports that women are also expected to be more communal, expressive, cooperative, and kind than men. Women have, over time, been expected to be the protectors of social harmony, which creates a continuous loop of cause and effect. The more protected and secure people are, the more likely they are to smile if smiling is socially acceptable. Social conditioning and gender roles kick in, pushing a demand for smiles-on-loop in order to make sure that everything is okay—even if it isn't.

Many cultures have positive interpretations of smiles, but there are some places where smiling is seen as deceptive or sinister. The language-learning platform Babble cites studies discussing the relationship between what's called "uncertainty avoidance" (UA) and cultural attitudes toward smiling. UA is based on the stability or instability of social institutions, and the lower the measure of UA, the less favorably a culture or society views smiling. According to Kuba Krys, a psychologist affiliated with the Polish Academy of Sciences, in countries with higher instances of corruption, smiling is viewed as dishonest.

Which came first—the expectation or the smile?

※

"Smile, Ashley! It can't be that bad!"

There are days when it is that bad. The stress is too much. The sleep too little. The work needs to be done. The pain—in my head, in my abdomen, wherever it is—is too much to handle. Sometimes, the world has just gone to shit, and even I, with my eternal optimism, just get fed up. Smiling isn't always worth it.

※

The smile has a somewhat convoluted history.

The Bible has only one instance of smiling named for what it is in the Old Testament. In the book of Job, about suffering at the hands of God, he is the one to flash the only smile before the birth of Jesus. In Job 29:24, it reads that Job "smiled on them when they had no confidence, and the light of my face they did not cast down." But even then, when the passage is cross-referenced across various translations, the smile fades in and out of this narrative. Sometimes Job smiles, sometimes he laughs, and in one instance, Job mocks the people looking at him. Out of all these translations, though, most of those who surround Job at this moment doubt his smile. Not even Jesus is described as smiling in the Bible.

In the book of Job, it seems as though smiling and suffering are not compatible, that we lack the capacity to feel multiple emotions at the same time. The sense of wonder associated with Job's story resonates with me; I understand the comments from those in awe of how often I smile even amid suffering. For me, a smile sometimes distracts from the reality of what I feel, what I experience, so that I don't have to explain or justify what I don't yet have the words or the energy to understand or communicate. Smiles defend and deflect.

Eastern religions, however, have a different point of view when it comes to smiling. Members of the Hindu faith living in India and much of Southeast Asia see smiling as part of being a good host and that smiling and hospitality go together. Although the original Buddhist religious texts do not mention smiling as a part of their narratives, some Buddhist figures are depicted as smiling as a way of reflecting the enlightenment Siddhartha Gautama attained. In his enlightenment, Gautama, now Buddha, found the path out of suffering and toward bliss, which left him smiling for centuries.

We should not always take smiles as a given, a certainty. When saved, the smile has the power to radiate outward across time and space.

✺

"Smile, Ashley! You look like your face is going to break!"

One of my signature characteristics has, for some of those around me, become so commonplace that not smiling is cause for commentary. When forcing that smile becomes too much of a task to handle, I let my true feelings decide the shape of my face. I can only fake a smile for so long.

There are days where I feel like my face, along with the rest of me, is going to break. I still put on a smile, but that smile never seems to be good enough for those who expect me to always smile. For them, a weak smile is worse than no smile at all.

✺

Women didn't always play the same part in the history of smiling.

For the longest time, smiling and laughing were considered immoral or sinful expressions of emotion for women. Essayist Amy Cunningham writes that the expectation, at least in European religious writings, codes of conduct, and art, was that women were not to display emotions, except for when women looked at their children with a serene expression that resembled how the Virgin Mary smiled at her child. I find this odd since Mary is never described in Christian texts as smiling at her child. The portrayals of Mary smiling at her child were to supposedly set up a contrast between Mary and Eve, who was viewed as sinful and wicked. Part of me wonders if they knew where this story was going in the years, decades, centuries to come.

For European upper-class women, society expected them to remain covered, not only as a way of preventing others from seeing their facial expressions but as a way of separating women from the rest of the world. Allowing women the opportunity to inspire others to sin or engage in a tensing of a small collection of muscles in their face would, no doubt, cause the fall of humankind. The only saving grace, it seems, was that women could smile at their children.

I would like to think that women's abilities to smile, to laugh, to express happiness through their bodies happen with the best of intentions. It turns out, though, that the path toward fire, brimstone, and eternal damnation is littered with smiles and laughter, a brief flash of either causing one to go up in flames unless a woman is a mother—which, given how the world has changed and continues to slip back in time, may not be a cause to smile if motherhood is something increasingly forced upon women again.

❊

"Smile, Ashley! You never smile anymore."

Psychologists who study smiling argue that if people, particularly Americans, would learn how to read smiles better, we would see that a smile can express a myriad of emotions.

I agree.

❊

My everyday smiling face is what most people know me for, which is not as exuberant as a genuine smiling face but sends a similar message. I also have the concerned smiling face, which looks like I'm probably still smiling, but with raised eyebrows, forehead tilted forward, and questioning what I just heard or saw.

Then there is what I call my serious face. This face first requires a sense of disbelief or critical concern based on choices or statements someone has made. Out of these feelings of disbelief or concern, or even sometimes general frustration, comes what friends describe as "The Face": head tilted to the left, lower jaw tucked in slightly. Eyebrows raised. My smile transformed into something between a pucker and a frown. After my face has settled into this arrangement, I linger for a long second or two before asking a question.

Some of my friends openly enjoy seeing my animated nature show itself this way. One of them unleashes a roaring laugh whenever "The Face" shows up. "It's just your face," she said, wiping tears from her eyes. "Your face just says it all."

※

Around the turn of the twentieth century, society started to see women smile in public more.

Advertisements with cheerful women selling the newest products, from drinks to home goods to cameras, appeared in public spaces. While the women in these advertisements were just gaining social acceptance because they—gasp!—shared smiles with a public audience, there was also a movement toward smiling as something that wasn't sinful but instead indicated wholesomeness. After all, if a camera can make the woman on a sign smile, then there must be something noble and good about having one of those cameras, right? The ushering of women's smiles into public acceptance also rode on the coattails of capitalism and a new era in history, showing us that our engagement with an economic system rooted in the exchange of goods and the exploitation of labor is as natural as smiling.

Slowly, as people imagined how they would smile with that new Coca-Cola or lamp or camera, we began to imagine what life would be like if we could also have *her*—the smile, the wholesomeness, the beauty put on display next to the stuff. The danger lies here in the equation of stuff equals happiness equals smiles equals beauty equals womanhood because if one factor in this equation falters, then the whole system may fall apart, which some would argue absolutely cannot happen.

After all, it is smiling women who are responsible for social harmony and stability.

⁂

"What's wrong, Ashley? Why aren't you smiling?"
   "What if I don't want to smile?"
   A pause.
   "You look so much nicer when you smile."

⁂

Cunningham, in her essay "Why Women Smile," writes about how other countries haven't been so keen on adopting the American smile.

Corporations such as McDonald's and Disney have tried. They set up camp in countries such as Russia and France, thinking that they could replicate the success these companies saw in the United States. But, as Cunningham writes, after setting up a new restaurant or amusement park, both of which are known as havens for blissful smiles, the American members of these teams sent overseas to launch these brands had a complaint—the Americans couldn't get the people they employed to smile to American standards.

With the ways in which American culture has changed, I wonder if I can blame them for not buying into our narrative.

⁂

Friday night video chat with my friends from college who live seven hundred miles away. I am in *a mood*. I need to vent.

After I've let it all out, one of the first reactions is to my lack of a smile. "You know it's bad when Double A isn't smiling. She's about to start flipping some tables."

My lack of smile not only upends social harmony but the furniture as well.

⁂

One of the most common places women are told to smile is in the workplace.

Inc Magazine shares the findings of a 2019 survey on women and being told to smile in the workplace. The results were surprising. They showed that 98 percent of women surveyed, representing a wide range of professions, had been told to smile at work at some point in their careers. Of the women participating in the survey, 37 percent reported that the most recent place they were told to smile was in the workplace, while 36 percent of women surveyed held senior- and executive-level positions within their companies, which made this group the most likely to receive these comments. Additionally, *Inc Magazine* reports that being told to smile at work had a direct relationship with feeling underappreciated, particularly if the advice comes from a boss who is also a woman.

But it isn't just from bosses and colleagues.

One instance comes to mind. When I was seventeen, I worked at the local McDonald's during the opening shift on the weekends. Because this restaurant was right off the highway connecting Akron, Youngstown, and Pittsburgh, the early-morning shift meant that a substantial number of our customers during those predawn hours were truck drivers. One such truck driver came in, his face, hands, and clothes smeared with oil and grease. He stepped up to the counter and, before ordering, asked me a question. "Why is your shirt a different color than the guy back in the kitchen?"

I explained that the color of our shirts denoted our leadership position in the restaurant and that my red shirt denoted that I was a crew trainer, the tier of employee between regular crew and management. "Oh, so you're like, in charge here or something?"

"Not really," I said.

The truck driver placed his order, a breakfast sandwich meal with a large strawberry milkshake despite the chill outside, and I bagged his order, all the while maintaining the smile I was expected to keep on my face for my nine-hour shift. I handed the man his order and, as I took a step back from the counter, said, "Thanks for stopping in! Enjoy the rest of your day!" I went back to work.

He lingered, unwrapping his straw as I kept busy behind the counter. After a few moments and sips of his milkshake, he waved at me as if he needed something. "Can I help you?" I asked.

The truck driver leaned over the counter. "You've got such a nice smile. I'd like to take you home with me if you know what I mean," he whispered.

I took more than one step back and felt my smile instantly fade. The truck driver made his way toward the door, winking and tipping his hat in my direction. I walked down the row of fry vats and toward the office, where my manager sat doing paperwork. She saw that something happened on the security cameras but couldn't understand why I walked away at that moment. She hadn't heard what had been said, and when I told her, nothing in her facial expression changed.

"What was wrong with that?" She glanced at the security camera screen and saw someone else walk into the lobby. "You've got a customer."

I was seventeen. The last thing I wanted to do was to wait on another customer, let alone smile. The differences in the comments about smiling, the suggestive one from a stranger and the subtle one from a manager, were dizzying, especially when my personal boundaries had been crossed and no one seemed to care. At that time, the nonresponse from my manager felt like betrayal. If she didn't get it, I wondered, then who would?

⁂

Cunningham writes that American women smile so often and in such a way that the Smiling Woman has become a uniquely American character type, something that isn't an inherent part of other cultures' gender roles.

While search after search for the Smiling Woman archetype returns two types of results—Cunningham's essay and scholarship on the mammy character that exists as a racist caricature—I wonder if this is true. Has the Smiling Woman become another archetype to add to our list? If so, how did that happen so quickly? In her essay, Cunningham writes that smiles have power, but American women too often deny that power in order to mask what we're really experiencing. Cunningham notes the oddity of how we control our faces in light of the work American women have done to secure control over other parts of our existence.

Is that how we got here? Given the way that the fight for women's rights has taken a drastic and dark turn backward since 2022, I'm beginning to wonder if sincerity is the most accurate way to measure the success of what Cunningham calls the women's movement. Instead of smiles and sincerity, maybe our metrics should look more closely at our rage, our anger, or, better yet, our actual freedom to control our entire bodies and not just pieces and parts.

⁂

"Smile, Ashley!"

Sometimes, when I hear those words, I simply walk away.

I think about the times I've been told to smile and how the minute intensity of each of those moments builds until the force cracks my personal space and threatens to overwhelm me. I've been smiling for so long that I can no longer separate the smiles that come naturally from the smiles that I have been socially conditioned to display on my face.

Granted, I have plenty to smile about: friends and family and foods that sustain me, flowers and words and the beauty of clouds. I have reasons to smile of my own volition. I can feel my pulse rising and falling and, when I focus, can hear the faint whistling of my breath as it passes in and out of my body. I am alive, which for me, is an opportunity to smile.

I can think of many reasons not to smile. Sometimes the pain of my condition stops me in my tracks. All I can do at that moment is breathe, deep and slow, and wait until it passes, the imaginary knife withdrawing from my ovaries. There are also days when I feel the fatigue, the anxiety, the mix of feelings and states of being swirling around in my head. It is all I can do to hold back the wetness of tears or the heaviness of sleep. A smile is not a thought that crosses my mind when my first impulse is to lay my head on my desk, despite it being barely noon, or to find a place where I can put a door or a wall between me and the rest of the world and think about how it is possible to just fall apart. In these moments, smiling not only feels like a lie, but one I cannot tell even for survival. Instead, the insistence on smiling in spite of everything feels like a forced conformity, a way of someone else continuing to deny who I am and how my body functions.

I can find more reasons not to smile when I watch or read the news, especially when there's talk about the need to further regulate access to birth control and women's health care, acting as though the card of twenty-eight tiny pills that sit in my otherwise empty soap dish on the bathroom counter don't have any other purpose besides preventing babies. I sit at my computer and type, time after time, about why access to women's health care should be a priority, about the years it took for me to receive a proper diagnosis, of the times when I have had to do my best to make it through the day despite feeling like the life had been drained out of me because I couldn't get the help I needed. And after the *Dobbs* decision in 2022, I find myself smiling less and less and raging more and more. With each new report of bans and restrictions and women whose lives have unnecessarily been put in danger, I want to scream until my throat has turned to shreds. *I am more than just a smiling face and a womb,* I want to tell them. *I am a whole person.*

These are times when I can pinpoint the reason I am smiling. In those instances, my smile is not a genuine smile, but instead, my smile is the one I've been conditioned to have on my face because that is what a lot of other people, even some of those who know me the best, expect from me. Smiling makes me approachable, not angry and scary. But there is still that expectation to smile because, after all, *it can't be that bad.*

Women are in danger! people reply. *It is that bad!*

Women are in danger! people reply again. *People could die because of this!*

It can't be that bad, the others repeat as women are suffering and being left to die in the parking lots of hospitals because of denied access to health care, to services they need to save their lives.

Women have died! people shout.

And yet—*it can't be that bad,* say those who insist that women are still protected after May and June of 2022.

In reality, it is that bad. And it will only get worse.

⁂

"Hello, Ashley. I saw your profile and was mesmerized by your smile."

Random stranger who, upon finding my profile on a dating website, tracked down my work email address to tell me about my smile.

I promptly deleted the email without responding.

⁂

There are days when I catch a glimpse of myself in the mirror and I cannot describe the expression on my face. It isn't a smile. It isn't a frown either. Instead, the corners of my mouth are casually pulled back in neither a smile nor a frown. Nothing else about my face has changed, but there is something reassuring me that I don't have to smile, that I owe no one a smile, and maybe, just maybe, it is time to take back those small muscles in my face from a culture that says yes, because you are who you are, you must smile.

You owe us your smile.

It can't be that bad.

It is in those moments where the cracks turn into breaks, and I can either walk away or stay a while to watch the crumbling. Sometimes, the crumbling has more power to it than the smile.

Not In Bed

I can tell when one is coming. It sneaks up behind me in a fit of confusion, right behind my eyes, prepared to settle in a blind spot.

When a migraine begins, I have found myself in any number of places: the grocery store, the classroom, on my couch, in a hotel room, or on the edge of my bed as I start a new morning. The first sign is a sense of fuzziness behind my eyes and under my forehead. The onset of my migraines makes the world intimidating, a place I have learned to prepare for when the grocery store suddenly gets confusing, when I can't handle the conversation in a classroom, or when I stand in front of the bathroom mirror in the mornings with my toothbrush in one hand and the toothpaste in the other, failing to make the connection between the two objects and our shared presence.

I don't remember a time in my life when I haven't had migraines or, at the very least, headaches. As a child, my mom's and my teachers' first responses were to have my eyes checked. One day at the end of a mid-October school day in third grade, my mom picked me up and took me to the eye doctor, the one inside of the Sears department store, to try on my new glasses with tiny versions of Snoopy and Woodstock printed on the frames. For a while, I felt like I had new eyes and a new head. I still got headaches, though.

My migraines got worse during my freshman year of high school, which fourteen-year-old me spent partially in bed after a cocktail of school, band practice, sports practice, and homework caused my brain to just stop. It felt as though my gray matter lost the ability to function. The muscles around my eyes spasmed, and all I could do was stay in bed with tears streaming down my face. I fell asleep at some point, only to wake up the next morning at six o'clock sharp and get ready for school, knowing that the new day would be a repeat of the one before.

The final verdict came after a school year of doctors, appointments, specialists, an EEG, a CT scan in a mobile trailer because the children's hospital was under renovation: chronic atypical migraines. At fourteen, I had a form of migraine typically diagnosed in women between the ages of thirty and fifty. This diagnosis meant not living the carefree life of my peers because I didn't know what triggered a migraine or where I would be when one hit. For a teenager, this meant constantly having that nagging worry in the back of my mind, always making sure that I had pain relievers with me, always cautious of what I ate or how much sleep I got.

What causes these migraines, the atypical ones—my migraines? The ones that don't follow the prescribed pattern of migraines but instead cycle through multiple phases at the same time?

"It could be any number of things," a specialist said. "It could be diet. It could be stress. It could be allergies. Or, she could just have what we call a 'migraine personality' that makes her more prone to migraine headaches than the average person." For over twenty years, I've tried to figure out what a migraine personality is, what parts of my character fall under the category of this semifatal flaw. The "migraine personality" is nothing more than a term from the early twentieth century to describe a collection of personality traits that may or may not cause migraines: being high strung, being a perfectionist, or being anxious or worried. Belief in the migraine personality also means believing that a person's character is fixed and remains unchanged throughout their entire life, which is another misnomer to say the least. I am some of these things: perfectionist, anxious, the worrier. My personality should not warrant this diagnosis, filed under the category of an antiquated theory that does not align with medicine or psychology or, even more so, my needs as a person in pain.

I've since thought of other potential reasons for my pain. The weight of my hair straining my head and neck. Hormonal imbalances. Vitamin deficiencies. Sudden changes in the weather. The fact that it's Tuesday. Poor karma from a past life. It could be any number of things that I still try to pinpoint. Even at fourteen, I knew there was no stopping, no taking days or a week to lie in bed until the migraine subsided. I knew I had to go to school and do exceptionally well so I could get the scholarships to help me pay for college.

From there, the need to continue, to persist, to pursue continued well into adulthood with the need to always be doing more to prove myself to be the person I say I am. To prove that I mean something. To prove that I am worthy.

When I mention to someone else that I live with migraines, the advice almost always comes in waves. Many people say they have migraines, too, and offer what works for them: caffeine, no caffeine, stimulant-based pain relievers, depressant-based pain relievers, eating this, not eating this, taking a hot shower, taking a cold shower, hot compresses, cold compresses, turning the lights on, turning the lights off, activating any number of pressure points. The list is longer than I can feasibly put in a piece of creative writing and could fill journals full of research. The reality, though, is that science has done so little research on a woman's body that we socially, culturally, and scientifically don't know enough about migraines to treat them since more women experience migraines than men. When women lose, we all lose.

I've also tried other solutions. Taking vitamins before bed. Haircuts. Yoga. Dietary changes. Different settings on my computer. Blue light filers in my glasses. Daith piercings in both of my ears to supposedly stimulate acupuncture points. My migraines still come and go as they please.

I was in college when I first read Joan Didion's essay "In Bed." It was the first time I had encountered another woman writing about her migraines. I was used to dealing with my migraines in private, but it felt like a different kind of private from what Didion describes. She is able to retreat in a way that allows her to rest, to allow her body the time and space to do what it needs to do until the migraine cycle comes to a resolution. Afterward, she is able to return to public life, talk about what ails her, *and have people listen*—something that many women don't have. Her experiences in "In Bed" manifest themselves in the way she responds to an age-old question: *Do you have headaches? Never? Sometimes? Frequently?* Didion herself checked *sometimes*, which she admitted was a lie.

I ask myself—how does one choose an answer to that question and still have a life to live? I wonder about the act of disclosure in these instances, about the assigning of blame and how much of my migraine diagnosis was shifted upon my personality and not a variance in physiology.

I cannot allow myself to simply go to bed when I have a migraine. Why do I force myself forward even when it feels impossible? Why do I struggle with letting my body rest when its equilibrium has been disrupted? Maybe, just maybe, this is about erasure. The reality of having my pain invalidated by those who can't see the source of my suffering, who don't understand the source of what ails me, keeps me from just going to bed when a migraine hits. We, as in American society, have placed so much weight on visibility in relation to pain that pain from a wound from war or a broken limb is somehow different, more worthy of existence, than pain without a cause that others can lay their eyes on. In retrospect, it makes sense that refusing to acknowledge my pain became a mode of self-preservation from childhood. I was taught to erase my own pain before I could fully understand what pain is capable of.

I also wonder if, in part, I am too stubborn to admit that I am in pain at all.

Stubbornness has its limits, though. When stubbornness runs out, I wonder if the worry about being made invisible, of being on the edge of erasure, motivates me to keep going.

Are there ways in which people have erased the existence of migraines? Medically—no. Socially—yes. Stories of women popping pain relievers and moving on with their lives, of waiting until they are so sick that it is impossible to go anywhere except to bed, of forcing themselves into routines of barring themselves from rest until the house is clean are so deeply rooted in our culture that some women, by virtue of place or historical moment or economy, find rest as the default response to any ailment impossible.

The maintaining of social harmony falls upon women.

I am somewhat to blame for my inability to go to bed when I have a migraine, for enabling this cycle to continue. I would like to think that I could ask for help and not feel guilty about it. I know the world will keep spinning if I don't answer this question or say *no, I can't*. But the fear of what happens after I emerge from between the sheets and blankets, the fear of being seen as unable to endure, the reality of my pain being erased because of something that is very real but very much unseen is too big of a thing for me to squarely lay the blame solely on myself. Blaming people for their pain is a much bigger issue for those whose pain stems from an invisible source, as if there were a prize to win for achieving a form of perfection whose standards are forever shifting. In a way, I wonder if the idea of the migraine personality is not an internal cause, but instead originates, lives, and breathes from outside of one's own head.

I know what it looks like when I simply cannot summon the strength to continue on due to every fiber of my being forcing me to *stop*.

After the second round of two Ibuprofen and even more water, my words blur in my head. It becomes harder and harder to string sentences together. My skin pales. Sometimes I feel feverish, while other times I get the chills. I physically slow down because, if I stand up too quickly, I feel as if I could pass out. If needed, I press on, often because I don't have a choice or a chance to escape yet. But in those moments, my frustration with my inability to function grows. Sometimes I am simply irritable. Sometimes I want to dig my fingernails into the closest surface as a way to displace the pain circulating through my body. At the extreme, I want to claw things off—my skin, other people's faces, the paint off the walls—because there is no way to escape what is happening to me on my terms.

I eventually find myself sliding underneath the blankets in a moment of surrender or at the end of the day. The lights are off. I will not spend days in bed, but instead hours. In those hours in which I escape to allow my body to do the work it was built to do, a world exists outside that continues. I think of Didion, who describes her migraines as a blessing. I wonder where the blessing is in all of this and who that blessing is intended for.

I don't think it is meant to be mine.

Erasing Memory of Skin

On the last weekend of a lower-Midwest September, the only place I am comfortable is in my shower, surrounded by barely lukewarm water. I feel grimy, sweaty, as if I can't escape the stuff that has accumulated on my skin. The sweaty feeling is partially due to the weather outside and, in part, due to me trying to counteract the heat outside by making my apartment as cold as I can bear it. Pictures from the repairman show the exhaust pipe from my air conditioning unit covered in ice, a solid tunnel of cold heading in the wrong direction.

As I stand under the showerhead, I wonder what else I try washing away. Grime, sweat, dust. Dead skin cells. The heat of September threatening to spill over into October. Memories of touch just out of sight. A love I thought I had but instead slipped through my fingers. In washing them away, I wonder, maybe I will be able to find some peace.

I run my purple sponge over the echoes of stretch marks and scars, so faded that I can barely see them anymore. I inch closer to the water flowing from the showerhead and look down at the rest of my body. The echoes of touch from that lost love linger, too, and I wonder how long they will last before the sound waves break against things more concrete than air and begin to disappear.

I wonder just how one does erase the memory of skin, echoes ringing through layers, remembered in cells.

※

Lately, I find myself drawn to Maggie Nelson's book-length essay *Bluets*, a collection of 240 loosely linked fragments that meditate on the color blue.

This is neither the first nor the only time this book has intrigued me, but there's something in Nelson's words that feeds a part of me attempting to push away an all-encompassing sadness.

Each time I sit or flop or collapse onto my couch and reach for *Bluets*, its slim volume lying on the back of my couch, I return to the same sections. Fragments 195–208. The first in this series that draws my attention is Nelson writing about displacement, wondering if sharing our thoughts in some ways displaces or replaces the original thoughts we had to begin with.

When I feel adrift—displaced from a healthy body, a partner, a lover—I wonder what my album of written thoughts would look like. *Is this a displacement,* I think to myself, *or is it simply a replacement?*

What is it, I ask myself, *that has been displaced? What am I supposed to replace?*

⁂

I wake up Monday morning, and I see the red scaly patches that sometimes appear in the corners of my chin. I have yet to figure out why they show up—I would find out years later that they are triggered by a food intolerance that aggravates my hormonal imbalance—but their tightness pulls at the edges, and I scratch. Picking at dried cells makes the skin underneath ooze, and the redness and plaque spread. Not far, but enough that I feel the discomfort. I fear that others can see it, too, but I can't stop myself from picking at it. The only remedy is to let the redness disappear so I no longer see the difference between normal and not, and once those boundaries fall apart, then I find myself starting to heal.

This time, though, was different.

⁂

It's been over twenty years since Dr. Gary Chapman published his book *The Five Love Languages,* which looks at the five general ways in which people express their love for others. Chapman was a conservative Baptist minister who developed this idea of love languages while providing marriage counseling to his parishioners. Although there isn't any scientific backing to his theories, pop culture has taken the ideas and run with them.

There must be a reason that Chapman's work has endured. Maybe it's that we see something of value in the ways in which we express our feelings, even if those expressions can lead to the destruction of the relationships we try so hard to build. Or maybe it's the idea that someone has demystified something that we, as people, have been trying to figure out for as long as humanity has existed. Just how do we coexist?

As I read through descriptions of Chapman's five love languages, I already know how I convey my feelings to others. I'm not fluent in gift giving, which often makes me anxious and develop multiple plans to find *exactly* the perfect gift, for which often there is no tangible match for the ideal I have concocted in my head. Nor do my feelings translate into the language of service by doing things for the person I love. I try, but I try too hard. Some of this makes sense, and yet so much does not.

✻

The next day, Tuesday, I scratch my forehead while getting ready for the day. As I pull my hand away, I inspect my fingernails. A stark white powder is lodged in the space between fingertip and nail.

It's not day-old makeup. That powder is my skin, so dry that my forehead is turning to dust. My skin screams for something, but, for some reason, my body and I no longer speak the same language. My skin cries, but I stand in the wind wearing earmuffs.

After class on Tuesday afternoon, I decide to spend my feelings, a complicated mix of dread and loneliness. I go to the local sporting goods store and buy the most expensive travel mug I've ever purchased, followed by a trip to Target to buy my favorite kind of tea that I only buy as a treat. I know what is happening. I am searching for comfort, that in my discomfort of screaming skin and a lonely heart, I need something to hold close to me and designate as "mine." Today that something is tea and a vessel to carry it in so the warmth doesn't slip through my fingers.

At home, I pour scalding hot water into the travel mug, one batch to rinse the inside of the purple and gray contraption out and a second to make tea. I know a sickness is coming on because I usually only drink hot tea when I'm not feeling well. I drop two tea bags in the mug. The herbal blend smells citrusy and spicy as it steeps and makes my apartment cozy. About a half hour later, I come back and take a deep gulp from my new mug, forgetting its promise to keep hot drinks hot for up to twelve hours.

I open my mouth as I sit my tea back on the kitchen counter to let the heat escape. My tongue feels scorched, its surface bearing the brunt of the damage on top of what I have already put my body through.

When I am under stress, I crave acid and heat. Instead of chocolate or wine or ice cream, I want hot sauce, acidic fruit juices, iced tea with obscene amounts of lemon. By the time I wake up Wednesday morning, I have consumed so much acid that the tip of my tongue and the insides of my cheeks are speckled with the hard, white ulcers of a diet out of balance. The tip of my tongue has three or four that make it difficult to speak without pain. Those ulcers, combined with the scalded tongue from my first sips of tea, make me wonder if I'm being told that what I need to say should not be said at all.

⁂

Eleven days after that sweaty shower and two days after buying the travel mug, I wake up to clues that I am about to have one of the worst migraines of my life. I find it difficult to string my thoughts together as I go about my day. My face looks paler than usual. My eyes have difficulty focusing, and, ever so slowly, the pressure in my head builds. My classmates that afternoon comment that I don't look well, that I just look worn out. A half hour into class, the pressure in my head is so great that I can't feel the touch of my hand I use to hold up my head. I suffer through the rest of my two-and-a-half-hour seminar, refuse a ride home from a friend, and I am in bed by four in the afternoon. I don't wake up until seven the next morning, oversleeping my alarm by an hour.

When I sit up the next morning, my skin screams. I don't know what is wrong with me, but I can't move without pain. I feel my stomach revolt as I try to sit at my desk long enough to send an email canceling the class I teach. I choke down some breakfast and barely force some orange juice down. This level of unwell reaches new heights. I go back to bed and sleep most of the weekend away, but no matter what I do, the physical pain in my skin refuses to quit.

I call the doctor's office Monday morning and ask for an appointment. The receptionist tells me that I have a pick of any appointment time after eleven that morning in twenty-minute increments. I pick an afternoon appointment that would allow me to still teach my morning class and hold office hours because I am stubborn if I am anything. By the time I get to the health center that afternoon, a piece of skin on the inside of my thigh has ruptured and is slowly oozing a thick, vile-smelling gunk that could only be described as having the smell of disease and boiled cabbage. This doctor says they're not equipped to help me here, my university's student health center, and that they've already called the emergency room at the university's women and children's hospital. "They're expecting you," she says. I hobble to my car with directions written on a notepad with some kind of pharmaceutical name printed on the top.

The physician's assistant in the emergency room confirms what the doctor at student health suspected: skin infection. The vile-smelling lump on my inner thigh is an abscess caused by the infection and was likely triggered by my massive migraine and all the time I spent in bed, under the blankets, with a body too overwhelmed to fight the infection off. As the assistant pokes and prods around the lump, I react to the various degrees of pain. A firm grip on one part of my skin near the abscess makes me dig my nails into the cushion-covered examining table. She sighs and shakes her head, telling the nurse that it's no wonder I'm in pain. As she drains and packs the abscess, she tells me she's in deep, measuring the now hollow pocket of skin in inches. "If you had even waited until tomorrow to come in," the physician's assistant says as she pushes more bandaging into the open wound, "this probably would've been an overnight stay. You would've most likely been septic."

Afterward, I get cleaned up and dressed in the clothes I wore to teach that morning. The nurse comes back with my discharge papers, a prescription for painkillers, and two more prescriptions specifically for skin infections. The nurse also hands me two creams: one to repair my skin and another to form a barrier to prevent further damage. I am free to go and slowly make my way back to my car, hoping that I can get myself home before the first round of painkillers really kicks in and numbs everything, skin and bones and mind.

I barely make it home in time and have to call a friend to take me to the pharmacy to fill my prescriptions. "Why didn't you call me sooner?!" she asks as we're standing in my living room and my foggy brain tries to remember where I put my phone. My friend touches my shoulder, directing me toward my phone in plain sight on the clear acrylic coffee table. The way I tense at the feeling of her touch on my shoulder gives a clear message that the painkillers only work so much.

"It's okay. I can do this," I say. I need to give myself the pep talk because my skin feels so foreign. I need something to be normal when, clearly, there isn't much normalcy to be had lately.

Chapman's fifth love language is the one in which I am most fluent, touch. I am a hands-on, interactive person who needs to feel the concreteness of the world around me. I learn best by touching and doing. I express love by holding hands, by snuggling on the couch and curling up next to someone while I sleep. In some ways, my skin's need to be touched and to touch others is barely satisfied, so much so that, when it isn't possible for me to give a hug or curl up next to a lover, I often find myself rolled up in blankets or picking the softest sweaters out of my closet so that sensation of fibers against my skin brings comfort.

When my skin doesn't cooperate, as it couldn't in that long shift from September to October, it's hard to speak one's native language when what I want to say is not what my body wants to hear. I felt untouchable, in need of cleansing in order to be able to speak that language again. Sometimes the effects of that language become impossible to erase, no matter how hard I scrub every inch of me.

I, too, ask the same question Maggie Nelson poses in those fragments I return to over and over again, wondering how and when do I decide to recover or to stay broken for as long as possible.

※

Fragment 203. Nelson has somehow moved from rivers to memory, from the Disney movie *Fantasia* to, in this fragment, drugs in the 1980s. But these moves are so graceful, so artfully balanced, that I don't mind that I am whisked from something natural to simulation to stimulant.

I wonder what else lives on in our systems forever, whether they be the highs of love or the stings of trauma, the curses of history or the ever stretching reaches of desire, that seep into our bones, settle in our marrow, and begin to bump against our cells as they are thought to be born anew but instead rising to the surface of our skin, banged and scarred and bruised.

※

While I am sick, I take a lot of showers. There is more at stake now. I am not only trying to wash the memories of the day to day from my skin but also the infection that makes me feel untouchable even though I am not contagious.

I finish my antibiotics on a Thursday morning twenty-five days after my air conditioning unit stopped working. I shed my pajamas, get ready for my morning shower, and as I look down at my stomach, there are small red spots on my skin. I wonder what they're from. Maybe I'm having a reaction to the new bottle of shower gel, but I still hop in the shower and wash myself with what could be the offending blue-tinted body wash.

Throughout the day, the spots spread. The skin on the palms of my hands bubbles up beneath the surface. Red bumps that don't itch or burn or ooze or hurt show up on my hands. A plaque-like rash appears on my abdomen under my belly button. I go home and cry because I want my skin to be back to normal. I look up my symptoms and call the pharmacy. I tell the pharmacist on the phone what I've gone through for almost a month and what I was prescribed. "Well, to be honest, skin rashes are a side effect of both antibiotics you were given. Since you've been taking both of those drugs together, this is definitely a reaction. It's harmless and should go away in a few days."

"Okay, but how do I treat it?"

"Benadryl and, if you think you need it, some hydrocortisone cream. To be honest, though, unless it's bothering you, leaving it alone works just as fine too."

I spend the rest of the weekend popping antihistamines and using hydrocortisone cream like it is hand lotion. The rash bothers me, as does the rest of my skin as of late, but not in the way that the pharmacist had in mind.

As I swallow another dose of allergy medicine and rub my body with cortisone cream, two more medicines that replaced the two antibiotics, skin repair cream, and barrier cream assigned to my infection, I wonder what it will take to erase other memories from my skin. Will I have to shed like a snake, rubbing myself against the ground until my entire outer layer is left behind, a delicate and crisp netting that used to contain me, but is no longer adequate? The thought scares me because I am terrified of snakes. I take every opportunity I can to hide from them.

I wonder if the only possible solution is to shed every piece of skin from my skeleton, epidermis all the way down to the tissues lying beneath. A complete reset, a new skin, seems to be the only way to completely erase what is haunting me.

A complete reset, however, is not possible without death. I, too, ask the same question Maggie Nelson poses in those fragments I return to when I'm trying to figure out how I'm supposed to navigate this new reality of being both broken and recovered, refusing to pick just one.

I suppose that I will learn how to refuse, to recover eventually. In the moment, though, I feel as if I am studying for a test for which there were no lectures, no readings, and I am left to figure out the answers. Alone.

※

On top of the scrubbing and infections and rashes and pain, my weight refuses to stabilize. By the time the rashes show up, I have lost a hair under twenty-five pounds in just ten weeks. My skin no longer fits me.

※

Chapman's theory of the five love languages doesn't go without criticism. The lack of scientific backing for Chapman's theories is problematic enough, given that popular culture at large places a specific kind of weight behind the five love languages to not only understand how we connect with one another but to also rationalize our behaviors that may bring relationships to an end, too. Instead of acknowledging that love—both for one's self and for others—is hard and takes work, too many people engage in the pseudoscience of love languages to end the talk instead of continuing the conversation.

Love languages, unlike any other linguistic system, are incredibly rigid and inflexible, so much so that critics argue they are too strictly defined to be practical. In Chapman's estimation, a person gets a primary and a secondary language—that is it, no more. There is no room for dialects, for evolution, for growth and change. Love languages are starkly defined without any room for gray spaces in between. A person can, at most, only be bilingual in the world of love languages, and that is the limit of the discourse. This rigidity also carries over into who is included in the theory of love languages to begin with; not only is there no room for multiplicity, Chapman's theory relies on excluding vast swaths of people. His theory doesn't consider people who are not white, who are not conservative, who are not Christian, who are not married, who are not heterosexual, who are not monogamous—there are more people excluded from Chapman's theories than there are included.

Perhaps the enduring quality of Chapman's love languages is that it reinforces structures that make small groups of people in power feel safe. By continuing to exclude on the basis on Chapman's rigid white, heterosexual, conservative Christian values, the love languages theory chooses to ignore that the simple act of skin-on-skin contact reverberates in an untold number of ways, some of which are not positive.

In the first edition of *The Five Love Languages,* Chapman outlines a case study of one of his parishioners, whom he names Ann, who seeks out advice as to how to handle her husband's cruelty. Instead of providing support for what was really happening, Chapman classified the husband's behavior as expressing his love language of physical touch and that the remedy for the husband's acts was for Ann to initiate sex more often and to keep her faith. After receiving pushback on his advice, Chapman revised the case study in later editions of the book to provide advice while still doubling down on the misogyny.

What Chapman never comes out to say in the case study about Ann is that her husband's behavior is domestic violence.

The problem with love languages is that they rest on so many ways of doing harm that we begin to believe the only way to love is through destruction. The problem with destruction is that we, socially and culturally, have taken this so far that "love" and hate have gotten tangled up in the rationale for that destruction; out of a duty to protect, we must destroy. Instead of refusing, instead of recovering, there can only be wrecking.

When will we learn this is not the only way.

❋

The last remnant of shedding my skin and what ails it is two bands of a thick, rough plaque, one on the inside of each thigh. I lightly scratch my skin to try to loosen them enough so they'll peel. My old skin comes off in chunks.

I wonder what all my body is trying to shed. The infection? The rash? The reaction to the antibiotics? Something else entirely? Maybe all four?

I inspect the topography of these pieces of plaque, some of which are tiny and some of which are almost the size of a dime. They're lumpy and bumpy and rough on both sides. Nothing about them is smooth or indicates an ease with which they formed. To me, their surfaces indicate trauma, internal and external. Something about my surface has noticeably changed. The ridges on the cap of the orange juice bottle dig in and hurt more than they did in the past. Hot dishwater is almost unbearable but necessary to get my dishes clean. I find myself scratching more than before.

I hold the pieces of my skin in the palm of my hand before throwing them in the bathroom trashcan. They are darker than my skin has ever been, and I wonder if it's the medicines or remnants of the infection or memories haunting me.

When I visit my family in Ohio for Thanksgiving, my skin is still shedding. Particularly, the skin on my hands refuses to stop peeling, but the pieces that lift themselves from the layers underneath become smaller and smaller each time a new layer of skin is exposed to the air. I see it as progress.

I have lived with my skin long enough to know what it does and has done. In light of the layers of cells and plaques, of memories infused in my skin, language and runes and the faintest essence of touches that made the world shiver, I wonder how much progress I can make until one of two things happens: I return to stability or dissolve.

※

I'm not sure if this new skin, young and tender, is a displacement or a replacement. Recovery comes slowly, like the creeping of the sunrise.

I'm still not sure if I have washed away what triggered the unease that accompanied all of this, and, if I have, it is not something that I am willing to share. Maybe my skin has simply shed enough—enough memory, enough infection—that it has sloughed that script off my body. Maybe it was all the showers. Maybe it was just simply that I never had a chance to hold on to whatever is no longer mine.

Small changes in the surface or the appearance of my skin cause me to worry. I still hear the warning about sepsis when I insist that whatever is ailing me is minor because I have now set more than one precedent for a serious ailment. Instead of being there—something to watch and touch and hold my body together—my skin requires more from me. Sometimes, it just whispers. Sometimes, it demands attention loudly.

I wonder if my skin will continue to be so sensitive, so vulnerable, forever. I wonder if impermanence includes what can't be seen. Permanence is too much to put together in that moment of heightened awareness of something like skin, something constantly creating and erasing itself. The memories, the sensations, the hauntings. I think about this as I recoil from the things that didn't used to make my skin hurt, as I shake my hand to try and rid it of that aggressive feeling of rawness, old and new.

Foot Traffic

It took me six months after its release to sit down and watch *Barbie*, the 2023 blockbuster film based on the iconic doll. Everyone around me thought I would rush out to see the movie, with the pink fantasy world and the supposed message of women's empowerment and how women can be anything and do anything they want.

The problem is that I'm not a movie person, which is why I didn't sit down to watch the movie until my sisters set up a movie night while I was visiting over Christmas.

Months later, I recall a portion of *Barbie* while walking down the hallway of my apartment and catch a glimpse of my battered Birkenstock sandals resting in a pile near the door. It was the end of another semester of teaching that felt increasingly exhausting. I so desperately wanted to scrub my apartment from top to bottom, to rid myself of the mess that had accumulated while I, at times, felt like I could barely keep my head above water as a single woman who had been taught and fully believed that she could do, well, everything.

Instead, my mind recalled *Barbie* and the moments that set up Stereotypical Barbie's adventure that would play out over the course of the movie. I sat down at my computer and replayed the fragments I could find on YouTube, starting with the scene where suddenly everything is not okay. Stereotypical Barbie is on the beach with all her friends having a great day in Barbie World; there is sand volleyball and watching the ocean, lifeguards to keep everyone safe, music to keep spirits high, and friends to make memories with.

But when Stereotypical Barbie steps out of her stiletto sneakers to join in on the fun, something unusual happens—her feet go flat. Her existential crisis that started with thoughts of death is suddenly paramount after talking about her fall and embarrassment with the other Barbies at the beach. Something must be done, they decide. Stereotypical Barbie must go see Weird Barbie, they all say, to see if her feet can go back to "normal."

❋

It's late January 2018, and I had been in a simmering existential predicament since the announcement broke two weekends ago. Payless, the shoe store, was going out of business, closing not only all its brick-and-mortar stores but its online presence, too. I looked at my go-to black ballet flats with the cute, tight pleats along the toe box and noted the holes in the bottom of the shoes. I have a knack for doing that. They weren't the first or only pair of shoes I had worn until there were multiple holes in them.

Central Missouri had been plagued with weeks upon weeks of blizzards, ice storms, and dangerously cold wind chills, so on the next reasonably decent weekend, I ventured out to the Payless at the local mall. I hoped to get some good deals, especially since their website advertised "up to 40% off!" as a thank you to the company's customers. In the back of my mind, I calculated how many pairs of my black flats I could reasonably buy. After all, if I could get a deal, what would be so bad about having a few extra pairs of shoes in my closet?

When I got to the mall, this store was *a mess*.

Though there was still some structure to the chaos, it was clear that the store had been picked over and, given the reprieve in the rainy weather outside, overwhelmed. One woman stood behind the counter and, after every transaction, took out her cell phone and snapped pictures of the receipts. I imagine the woman behind the counter sent them to her boss, who may have been keeping track of sales figures on their day off or while attending to other business. Another young man ran frantically around the store, reaching for boxes on the top shelves and helping customers find what they needed. I slid my way into the store undetected and started to look around.

I braced myself as I looked at what was left of the furry moccasins I had just discovered around Christmas, setting myself up for the disappointment that I knew would soon hit me. Seeing nothing in a size ten on the shelf, I pulled a box marked nine and a half off the shelf and tried squeezing my foot into the dusty rose slipper shoe, the kind just soft enough to wear around the house but looked just enough like an actual shoe to wear out in public. My foot would only go so far. I moved on and wondered if there was even anything left for me to look at.

❁

In the interest of full disclosure, I should put this out there.

I. Hate. Shoes.

I have hated shoes for as long as I can remember. From fifth grade until my senior year of high school, I wore a size nine and a half wide, women's. I don't remember an age where I wore shoes in a child's size; I know I did at some point, but those times were before I was actively aware of these kinds of things. High school sports were not kind to my feet, and by the time I put on my cap and gown for graduation, I was sliding my feet into a size ten wide. When the shoe industry decides that a woman who wears anything bigger than a nine must either be elderly, frumpy, or solely wear black nonskid work shoes because her feet have been categorized as excessive and unladylike, it is easy to hate anything that goes on her feet. Including socks, which at a size ten, either just barely fit my feet or are so big that they slide off.

In some ways, I did not inherit a knack for things like shoe shopping, for wearing makeup, or really for buying things that are meant to accompany the clothes I wear. My mother has never owned makeup and, for the longest time, had three pairs of shoes: her good sneakers, her working-in-the-yard sneakers, and her black nonskid work shoes. At one point, my mom had a fourth pair of shoes, a pair of Mary Jane-esque dress shoes to wear when it seemed that, every summer, someone was graduating or getting married, but they have since disappeared. Her mother never wore makeup and only wore tennis shoes; Grandma's eczema and diabetes made many of those decisions for her. My grandma on my dad's side of the family wasn't much different but not because of her health. Along with the color of my hair and eyes, I've inherited a strong tendency toward the practical instead of the pretty. I sometimes wonder if this is a by-product of my heritage, descending from a Midwest American lifestyle that required everyone to pitch in with the work of keeping people alive. Practicality meant survival. That's not the life I live now or have ever lived, waking up before dawn to milk cows and work a farm, which makes me think about why I pause in shops and at window displays and browse online to look at the pretty things but don't easily take the steps to make them mine.

In the movie, Stereotypical Barbie soon finds herself climbing a set of winding stairs to Weird Barbie's house. Weird Barbie, up until this point in the movie, has been characterized as the sage-like outcast who was played with too much in the "real world," where Barbies are toys and not living, breathing beings.

As Stereotypical Barbie explains to Weird Barbie what happened to her—the flat feet and thoughts of death—Weird Barbie explains how, essentially, there has been a disturbance in the barrier between the fantasy world where Barbies live as people and the "real world" where Barbies are toys and companions. To solve the problem of Stereotypical Barbie's flat feet, Weird Barbie presents a choice to be made, symbolized by two shoes. Stereotypical Barbie can either stay in the fantasy world and continue to let the changes impacting her body happen—symbolized by the pale pink stiletto—or she can go to the "real world" to mend the rip between the two spheres of existence. The real world is symbolized by a much nicer and newer pair of Birkenstock sandals that look just like mine, the ones resting in a pile by my apartment door when I remembered this movie.

At first, Stereotypical Barbie immediately chooses the stiletto. I don't blame her; sometimes it is easier to live in a fantasy and forget about how brutal and cruel the "real world" can be to women, even though Barbie has a lot going for her that protects her from the ugliness of the world that is intruding on her life of beach parties, fun, and women's empowerment. Weird Barbie counters, saying that there isn't a choice; Stereotypical Barbie must choose the Birkenstock, the "real world," to heal her flat feet, cellulite, and thoughts of death.

The statement made by the choice between stilettos and Birkenstocks is not lost on me. Both shoes have their drawbacks. Stilettos sexualize and damage the bodies of those who wear them regularly. Despite their comfort and durability, Birkenstocks take a long time to mold to the wearer's feet and, even then, aren't the best since they force a person's toes to curl in unnatural ways to keep the shoes on. But the Birkenstocks represent a conscientious choice that isn't a choice; a woman can choose beauty—the stiletto—or power—the Birkenstock—but cannot have both. To have power, Weird Barbie implies, one must sacrifice beauty and the fantasy of protection that comes with it.

There is a cultural heritage, too, that not only emphasizes women's shoes but also their feet. When someone with a large shoe collection comes up in conversation, Imelda Marcos, the wife of Philippine dictator Ferdinand Marcos, comes to mind. So does Carrie Bradshaw, one of the main characters in the hit television series *Sex and the City*; her collection of high-end designer shoes is believed to have cost $40,000 at the time the show was set. Then there are the "Chicks with Kicks," the Peters sisters from South Florida who collectively own over six thousand pairs of sneakers that have an estimated worth of over $2 million. As I dig more and more into the relationship between women, their feet, and what they put on those feet, the missing link of how economics plays into the equation becomes more and more clear. Not only is there an absurd financial value placed on women's feet and what they wear on them, but the amount of money spent on shoes and footwear becomes not only a status symbol but also a marker of femininity, too. To be considered feminine, a woman—by social standards—must invest a hefty sum into what she does with and puts on her feet. By this measure, femininity is not just social or cultural but a financial marker of one's identity, too.

But there's more to this than just shoes. Women and their feet have been the focus of cultural practices for centuries. Women in China underwent foot binding for centuries, a practice that was still in place up until 1950. Foot binding is a practice where women had bones in their feet broken, their toes curled under, and their feet bandaged to keep them small. This altered the way women walked, too, forcing them to take tiny steps, creating a frail-looking gait. In India, it is common practice to touch the feet of elders to indicate respect and humility. The ebb and flow between reverence and harm for the parts of the body that allow for mobility is enough to make heads spin, especially when thinking about who is revered and who is harmed.

More broadly, society and culture have made links between the size of women's feet and their level of attractiveness. Anthropologist Daniel Fessler writes in *Scientific American* that foot size has long been associated with attractiveness in many cultures, although Fessler notes the correlation does not make sense from an anthropological or evolutionary standpoint because larger feet would, in theory, mean that those women are more stable on their feet and less likely to fall while pregnant. That theory would suggest that women with bigger feet should be more attractive than they are portrayed to be in some non-Western, male-dominated societies. It is in these cultural contexts that biology and fantasy are both at odds with one another and are yet forced to coexist.

⁂

I looked at the pairs and pairs of high-heeled shoes that lined the store shelves. There were wedges left over from summer—who knows how to walk in those things anyway?—and espadrilles galore. I glanced at the black nonskid work shoes that I'd spent thirteen years of my life buying and replacing when I worked fast food to put me through college and two graduate degrees. Boxes and boxes of riding boots that I knew I could never squeeze into because, as my dad says, I have the calf muscles of a professional football player. I guess that's what walking around college campuses all day will do for you, but the comparison to a professional football player unnerves me. I don't want to be a professional football player. I want to be me.

Come on, shoe store—were there no black flats to be found?

I prefer to think of my muscularity as a result of constantly having to stand on my tiptoes to reach almost anything. To me, it indicates a sense of independence, of self-sufficiency, that I can use the body I have to move through this world without having to rely on other people to do things like grab groceries off the shelves above eye level, which considering my height, is an awful lot of things. Instead of thinking about the things right above my feet as a way of de-emphasizing my femininity, I would much rather think about how those muscles emphasize a stronger sense of self than whether my body conforms to the expectations of what a woman's feet and legs should look like.

⁂

Shoe manufacturers also contribute to the mistreatment of women's feet. The dangers of wearing high heels for prolonged periods of time have been known for a while, and are mainly due to the angle that women force their feet into so they can wear the shoes, causing all kinds of pain and altering the way a woman walks. Fessler writes that, on top of the damage that heels inflict on a woman's body, heels alter a woman's gait in a way that Western societies view as sexy and feminine. When women walk in heels, they take smaller and more frequent steps and rotate and tilt their hips more while bending their hips and knees less. The ways in which walking in heels makes women appear more attractive, by emphasizing a person's breasts, butt, and hip rotation, not only break women down by causing physical damage to their bodies but also reduces them to parts that others have sexualized.

Additionally, Molly Longman, a wellness reporter and distance runner, reports for *Refinery29* that women's sneakers aren't designed for women's feet. Women's feet and men's feet are shaped differently, but many leading manufacturers of sneakers use molds of men's feet to design women's shoes. Not only are women's feet shaped differently, but the bodily mechanics of women running are different from that of men running, which causes differences in injuries, as well. Women's feet tend to be flatter and wider in the forefoot, or the part of the foot by a person's toes, and narrower in the heel than men's feet. This also changes the mechanics of how women move, meaning that women are more likely to suffer from instability of the pelvis, patellofemoral pain syndrome, and stress fractures. Men, on the other hand, are more likely to experience problems with tendons and knee cartilage. In an interview with Harvard researcher Dr. Casey Kerrigan, Longman walks us through the shoe-making process and the latter's failure to find a sneaker that fits her feet without causing an array of injuries. Kerrigan notes that men and women suffer different kinds of running injuries with an increasing amount of those injuries resulting from poorly designed shoes.

In other words, women have two choices when it comes to their feet. Women can either wear shoes that damage and further sexualize their bodies, or women can wear shoes that masquerade as offering a better sense of comfort, but in doing so, risk moving in ways that are perceived, as Fessler writes, as being more masculine while wearing shoes that were most likely not designed for a woman's foot.

❄

I think back to the illusion of a choice that Weird Barbie offers Stereotypical Barbie in the movie. Pick the stiletto and remain in a fantasy world where everything is fine and women are happy and successful or pick the Birkenstock sandal and be a part of the "real world." For Stereotypical Barbie, this was meant to solve her existential crises of flat feet, cellulite, and thoughts of death that result in burnt waffles. For Stereotypical Barbie, the warning from

Weird Barbie of becoming soft and mushy and "complicated" means having the illusion of choice between a "regular life" and knowing the truth.

Unfortunately, for those of us who are not Insert-an-Adjective-Here Barbie, the illusion of having a choice is the truth, the reality, and the "real world" Stereotypical Barbie has to experience in order to get her body back. The choice itself is what is actually the fantasy.

⁂

There is a reason why I couldn't find the furry moccasins, the riding boots, or any shoes in my size. Most shoe manufacturers start to reduce their offerings—or stop offering shoes altogether—around a size nine. BBC News cites several reasons for this, most of them having to do with the production of shoes. As more and more shoes are made in Asia, with many of them also being designed in Asia, outsourcing has caused shoe sizes to shrink. The cost of manufacturing and shipping larger shoes increases as well. Aesthetics also plays a role because, like many other notions we've internalized to be true, smaller shoes look prettier than bigger shoes.

After all, look at how tiny Barbie's shoes are.

⁂

I have yet to understand the association of a love for shoes with femininity. Studies have shown that women will purchase, on average, 270 pairs of shoes in their lifetimes, each pair costing around $53. I can't even think of 270 shoes that I have liked enough to consider taking them home. My $65 pink-and-white Adidas athletic shoes were relics from my sophomore year of college in 2006. Those survived until mid-June 2019, when the bottom of the left shoe fell off on my way to hear the governor of Ohio speak at a summer leadership program I taught for. Society has all sorts of "rules" associated with what women wear on their feet and when and how that feel so unnecessary to me. Rules for shoes at work, rules for shoes before and after certain holidays, rules for when in the day a person should buy shoes, rules for *how* to buy shoes—to me, this is borderline crazy. It's not hard to find pages and pages of rules for buying and wearing shoes on the internet, but so many of these rules are dependent on their followers having the time, money, and ability to commit to adhering to standards of fashion and society. Not to mention a whole bunch of other factors that contribute to how a person thinks about, purchases, and wears shoes.

The funniest part of all the rules about the shoes we put on our feet is that shoes are a garment meant to protect a vulnerable part of our bodies, the ones who are constantly at risk of an injury or a mess. What is even more concerning is that, as time goes on, the rules meant to protect the vulnerable people attached to those vulnerable body parts are continually eroded, forcing us into worlds increasingly unsafe, dangerous, and not meant for us.

This is where I want to ask Stereotypical Barbie why the stiletto was her first choice when the illusion of what she has is becoming increasingly grainy and distorted.

❊

In the store, I finally spotted the familiar red-and-white box. I grabbed two pairs of my flats off the shelf, which I could justify since, at 40 percent off, it was almost like getting a pair for free.

As I made my way to the register, I took one more glance at the furry moccasin slippers, just in case someone had put back a pair in my size. No such luck. As I stood in line and waited to pay, parents tried to corral toddlers and small children into the kids' section to have their feet sized. Older women shuffled around the store, looking at earrings and commenting on the deals they found. Handbags and matching shoes sat on shelves at the end of each aisle. The bright fluorescent lighting shined off the white walls and fixtures in a tempting way. I imagined if I listened closely, I could hear the remaining merchandise whisper, "Buy me!" I wondered how long these two pairs would last before I, once again, destroyed them.

When the cashier rang up my shoes, I added two pairs of cushion inserts to my total—which, I thought to myself, were useless since they would each only last about a month—and thought that, well, if these were the last of these shoes I ever wore, I might as well take care of my feet. I swiped my debit card and gathered my bag to walk out of this shoe store for the last time. I caught a glimpse of the cashier taking a picture of my receipt before she called on the next person in line. It's as if society and culture didn't have enough documentation regarding women, their feet, the rest of their bodies, and what has been done and what we keep doing to them, that the addition of a picture of my receipt was needed as proof that yes, someone was here buying shoes. I felt like the picture of my receipt, along with all the other pictures of receipts I saw the salesperson take that day, only further confirmed notions about women that I, quite honestly, didn't want to be a part of. I just wanted to pay for my shoes and go home.

⁂

The thing about the choice presented in the *Barbie* movie is that there isn't actually a choice for Stereotypical Barbie to make. This moment in the movie—stiletto or Birkenstock—is the point where Stereotypical Barbie enters the "real world" and has to face the facade she's been living under as it crumbles. Despite the illusion of having a choice, Stereotypical Barbie doesn't have one. Instead, Weird Barbie uses the stiletto and Birkenstock to show her that some of the things she enjoys about Barbie World only exist in the fantasy life she lives. If Stereotypical Barbie continues to live this fantasy, she's doing a disservice to the ideals of the world she lives in while ignoring the reality of the women she and her friends were meant to empower.

But there's a reason beyond the plot of the blockbuster movie that Stereotypical Barbie has to face this realization in a fantasy world. Despite all the glitz and glam and opportunity that the pink stiletto offers to Barbie—the only thing that will change about her world is her flat feet and cellulite—too many women in the "real world" don't have the choice of the pink stiletto. They also don't have the choice of the Birkenstock.

All they have to choose from is their bare feet, trying to protect their vulnerabilities in a reality that increasingly lacks the necessities to keep them safe while still emphasizing that women are being protected. Even when they aren't.

That is what I think too many of us missed while watching Weird Barbie do splits and marvel at flat feet while her animatronic dog poops on the floor of her house atop the hill, leaving a mess for someone else to clean up.

⁂

I never wore the shoes I bought that day.

Payless started its going out of business sale just after I had bought myself a birthday present: a nice and expensive pair of shiny rose gold flats I found online. I had *never* spent that much on a pair of shoes.

But my feet felt so much better in them. Something about the way they molded to my feet made me want to keep wearing them, to rearrange my whole closet so I could maximize the number of outfits I had that would coordinate with rose gold flats. Never mind that it was January and the ground outside was wet and muddy with the remnants of snowstorms that weren't a very distant memory. For the first time in my adult life, I actually liked a pair of shoes in a way that I still can't explain. Maybe, I think as I revisit this memory and still see the rose gold shoes on my shoe rack in my bedroom, this is the closest I can get to what I would answer in response to Weird Barbie's choice in the movie; if I can't have the pink stiletto world and the Birkenstock world increasingly wants to push women farther and farther to the side, a rose gold ballet flat may be the only compromise available— with a steep cost.

Those black flats? Well, they sat on the shoe rack in my bedroom until the pandemic winter of 2021, still wrapped in white tissue paper with "American Eagle by Payless" stamped on it. I found myself in a fit of cleaning and purging my living space because there comes a point where small spaces contain too much *stuff*. Living in as small of an apartment as I did, clutter builds up quickly enough that, by the time that I realize clutter isn't just clutter anymore, the walls feel like they're starting to close in. I only have a limited amount of space in which to live, so I am regularly evaluating just how many objects I really do need in my home.

I started pulling pairs of shoes off the shoe rack. The heels I'd bought from Payless shortly after I graduated from college and hadn't worn in five years went into the donation bag. The Old Navy flip-flops, too. A pair of shoes that kind of looked like Keds sneakers but that I don't remember buying went into the bag. I picked up the red-and-white boxes that had sat for so long that, in my hands, they felt like the dust had not only collected but fused into the cardboard itself.

I opened the lid and looked at the shoes, lying in their tissue paper, waiting for someone to wear them. The shoes I'd bought just in case. These were flats that failed to make my gait sexier. They were practical: function over fashion. More and more knowledge of what shoes try to do to my feet gathered as I remembered that my shoes were the first thing I kicked off when I walked in the door of my apartment. That I would rather feel grass or carpet or even dirt touching the bottoms of my feet than the sole of a shoe. The dust-infused boxes at the bottom of my shoe rack reinforced that

I hated shoes, those objects that not only felt like a restrictive nuisance but were also made for me in a way that prompted me to spend money. They were not made for my body and the way it moved.

Unfortunately, I thought to myself as I took the shoes out of their boxes and put them in the donation bag, I am not the person for these shoes. They might be for someone else's feet but not mine.

That's Great

I sat across the table from the first guy I dated in a long time. Years, in fact. This was our second date, lunch at a local restaurant known for their biscuits. At this point, lunch was slowly turning into an all-afternoon event, but I didn't mind.

"And like I've told them, if I get married, that's great. If I have kids, that's great, too. Those things just aren't important to me," he said.

I don't know how we got to this moment in our conversation. We were talking about our families. My stomach tightened at the word *kids*.

It's not because I don't want kids. I do.

It's not because of what I ate. I've eaten this meal more than once.

It's because I didn't know how to respond. Granted, the second date was early to talk about that level of commitment. Really early.

I noticed I had stopped breathing. In that moment, every idea I had to continue the conversation disintegrated. This was not the first time I arrived at this decision: to tell or not to tell?

The truth is—I don't know if I can have kids. My disease can cause infertility. Oftentimes, women don't know they have polycystic ovarian syndrome, PCOS, until they try and try and try to get pregnant and don't conceive.

Potential infertility is the least of my worries when it comes to having children. At least, its place on my list of worries has shifted in the five, not quite six, months since the Supreme Court officially handed down the *Dobbs* decision in late June 2022. With PCOS, I am five times more likely to miscarry, and depending on which state I live in, when—because I feel that certainty in my bones—I miscarry, my access to appropriate and necessary medical care rests on how far a state's legislature has taken abortion bans.

That's because the medical procedures meant to help my body release what could have been my child are classified as abortive treatments. The hold I have on my breathing releases, and I feel my lungs do their job again. I maintain polite eye contact. I smile. I hope that the pause in the conversation hasn't reached an awkward length. The server stops by our table and asks if everything is okay. My date says yes, despite not knowing that I am sitting across the table contemplating having children, where I live, and if the combination of his wants and my realities could kill me.

A thought I hadn't considered before crossed my mind. It's too early to think about marrying the man sitting across from me, even if I'm already very smitten. It's too early to think about having children with him. But for a split second, I wonder if he would be the one I wanted beside me when that inevitable moment happens, when my body could no longer sustain the creation of another life. Is he the person—to come running or answer the phone when I'm undoubtedly screaming, to be the rational presence in the emergency room, to hold my hand as I wait for this nightmare to pass, to stand up for me when doctors and legislators say *no*, to make sure I get the care I need, to call my family and hold the phone to my ear?

I hate entertaining this thought. The fact that this disease completely changes how I think about motherhood makes my jaw clench. Instead of miscarriages and abortion bans, I want to contemplate baby names. I want to think about what it feels like to be pregnant. I want to imagine the people my possible future children could be and how I am going to teach them that always having a childlike sense of awe, wonder, and love is a good thing.

My heart wants to know that there will be a time when it won't ache when I shop for a baby shower gift or cry as I slide the card in its envelope, thinking *this may never be me.*

I want these to be my choices, and not the matter of life or death kinds of decisions either.

The time has come in our conversation for me to respond. If I stay silent any longer, a self-conscious awkwardness will creep in, possibly giving either of us a reason not to suggest a third date.

"Yeah, I mean, those are big decisions to make. Marriage and kids aren't for everyone." I take a sip of my iced tea to send a signal that I would rather talk about something else.

One of the servers makes rounds of the dining room to close the blinds. The winter sun has started to set and makes the light and airy space feel smaller. I wonder how my date's comment will forever change how I think about dates. Because of my body. Because of this disease. Because of how there are people who don't understand that having a choice is so much more than control.

But it's only the second date.

It's only the second date.

To Gaze

A salesman stands at the door where I work, saying that he is in the neighborhood and asks if I have a moment to talk about ordering office supplies. He is good at what he does. He has an answer or response for every statement I make about being satisfied with our current system, which is going to the store and buying supplies as we need them. When he responds that his company could do that for us, he looks me dead in the eyes. After the second or third time, I wrap myself in my sweater and fold my arms across my chest.

Being seen unnerves me. I'm not used to the glances or long stares. I am more comfortable as the behind-the-scenes person who takes charge not by being in front but by making sure everything else also remains unseen by working properly. Being seen, being the object of someone else's gaze, puts me on high alert. Knowing that my body takes up space, knowing that my body has a disease that causes it to function differently, knowing that my body has experienced violence from those who are not supposed to betray me sets off warning signs that trouble may be brewing. It is at this climax, this turning point where potential energy morphs into something else, into actualization, that I must make the decision to be seen, be the object of one's gaze, or be safe and unseen.

I think of an art exhibit I saw a few years ago in Cincinnati about a piece inspired by Laura Mulvey's essay that named a particular way of seeing. *Medusa,* created by South African artist Frances Goodman, discusses how the gaze works, a way of reducing women to the level of a passive object to create security in the sense that men are still in control. The sculpture ponders the things that women do to make their bodies more pleasing and reassuring.

The results of the artist's work were monstrous. Goodman assembled thousands of used acrylic fingernails in the shape of tentacles reaching out of the museum wall. Each nail was a different color and had a different pattern. Some were rounded and smooth, some squared off, some long and pointed as if to invite a second look but only from a safe distance. Together, the nails curled and twisted, stretched and recoiled, reached out to be touched as lovers do, while also folding into themselves as one might do when in the depths of an uncontrolled spiral.

I got my nails done regularly when I was younger. The acrylic ones, like those molded into tentacles. It started with junior prom, and I kept getting them filled and painted and buffed down, a new look meant to invite a glimpse every two weeks. The cost was significant for a high school student working fast food for six dollars an hour; one manicure was twenty-five dollars. The smell of chemicals made me lightheaded. I was often sweaty from practice or smelled of hamburgers after work when I walked in for my appointment. After I had the nails put on, I needed to learn how to do almost everything with my hands all over again.

But each compliment made me feel more seen, more favorable as something to be looked at. "Your nails are so cute!" they would say. When I walked into the salon missing one, two, sometimes three nails, I apologized to the woman who did them. "I'm sorry. I'm just not good at these girl things. I'm trying."

After a while, the struggle to keep up with the nails in addition to everything else I was supposed to do felt ridiculous. When the nails finally came off shortly after my high school graduation, the damage was done. If someone warned me about what this process would do to my natural nails, I can't remember. My natural nails were brittle and ready to break when bent just the wrong way. The chemicals in the acrylic ate away at them, just as being seen—or not seen—ate away at me.

The damage of the gaze runs deep. It chips away at most of the layers of how I compose my sense of self, especially in the months after I was told that my body, the only one I have and that I had been taught will and should behave and look and act in a particular way, the one that never could and never would live up to impossible expectations because it just can't, the one that didn't necessarily fit the patriarchy's expectations of what is normal and natural, that my body was not only different but in a dangerous way if I didn't work to try to control this disease.

It is here that I can count the ways I've already damaged my body so that myself and others would see my body as being normal and natural. The casualties—the parts of my body I tried to tame or fix or, worse yet, used to take out my frustration—add up as does the body count in war. My nails, the restrictive diets that left me in near constant states of faintness that never really worked, the scars from the razor blades, the need to apologize, even the way my body tenses when anyone outside a small circle of people touches me. To please others, my sense of self sometimes feels eroded and worn down, corners bent and some pieces not quite fitting together the way they used to, some parts shoved so far down into subconsciousness that I've found ways to put what remains back together so that it appears nothing is missing. If I am to survive, I must protect what is left before I disintegrate into shards, reaching out to be reassembled as a warning.

Like the art piece in the museum.

Like the nails I no longer have done, let alone paint myself.

Like the choices I make about makeup, hair, clothes—they're all ways that I make myself seen just enough that I exist as a human but not as an object.

Like the sweater I wrap around myself as I talk to the salesman at my door.

I know this is a defense mechanism. I know that this salesman is simply doing his job, but when being seen, being on the receiving end of a gaze, being someone who has felt the force of not being a natural and normal object that makes certain men feel unsafe and insecure in their masculinity and patriarchal status, being so tired of making those split-second decisions to determine what kind of gaze is safe and what means having violence directed at me, being a microcosm of all these things becomes too much, making myself less seen is a sigh of relief.

I wrap myself in my sweater and fold my arms across my chest, straightening myself to return to the good posture that had been reinforced in me time and time again. "I'm sorry, sir, but we're happy with what we already have here," I said.

But Do They Know?

The video on my phone stares back at me, even though the woman being silently interviewed—my settings have all videos muted—doesn't make eye contact with the camera. She sits at a microphone, her skin

brown,

her head

covered,

her nails

painted.

The closed captioning shows that she speaks of her femininity, her softness, of how people don't want

her.

She wants to date, to have people interested in her as a lover and a possible partner. I don't know too many more of the specifics, but the story of a woman feeling like she isn't wanted repeats itself when, every so often, another woman is thrust into the limelight of the court of internet opinion because she is different. Because this woman has facial

hair.

I make a mistake and look at the comments, a toxic space on social media. I am aware that I have my own stubble growing on my face. I shouldn't have looked at the conversation following the post. The comments are ugly; the mildest focusing on her

> fertility

while others advise her on hair

> removal

and some even suggest that her place is in the

> circus

implying

> she is a freak.

My discomfort hangs in the air like the central Missouri humidity we had earlier that week, an unofficial marker of spring—of renewal and rebirth weighing heavily on the air that keeps us alive, keeps us

> human.

My discomfort is that too many people don't see women or people with uteruses as

> human.

They only see us as objects to

> desire

to

> claim

to

> control

to

> suppress

because we are

> different

and the system was meant to grant humanity to some people and not others, and we live in a world where people who have certain beliefs keep changing the rules, wanting more

signatures

to get issues on the ballot and more

transparency

while they make it increasingly difficult to know what our government is doing while working to

separate

us based on distinctions that are completely

subjective

and

constructed

while they say that they are simply trying to

protect us

and operate under the guises of

Safety

and

Patriotism

and

Family Values

to protect their humanity while continually degrading ours. For those who are crying for more bans, more regulation, more black and white at the expense of burying gray under piles of laws and regulations and unnecessary outcries, a woman couldn't possibly have

facial hair

because that's not what we socially and culturally associate with women. That's not what we're told is supposed to be

right

or

natural

even though we, as a culture, have made these standards up for ourselves.

If a person is a woman, she is supposed to look a certain way, behave a certain way, exist in a certain way, adhering to a very narrow interpretation of one specific religion that, for those who believe, is the only way to understand the universe. Anyone else is

dangerous

and

immoral.

For women who, like me, who have polycystic ovarian syndrome (pcos,) we don't always have a say. We can't control everything our bodies do and we haven't done anything wrong—except for existing. No one chooses to have a medical condition that alters not only the chemistry and the physicality of the one body they'll ever exist in. The label of

different

only serves to remind us that people have come up with one set of rules that refuse to budge to keep certain groups

comfortable

at the expense of the

humanity

of others.

⁂

⁂

✷

✷

I empathize with the woman confined to the small frame of her interview. As people in the comments issue armchair diagnoses of PCOS, the same medical condition I live with day in and day out, I can begin to understand the feeling of not being wanted. Of being told your body is

wrong,

that your bed is

empty

after a partner has decided to move on, when you reveal your

body

to the world in places of judgement:

the doctor's office,

the gym,

the first tense moments of physical intimacy,

the dressing room at the store,

trying on clothes

too small

for a body

too big

to possibly be

loved

in a world where the loudest voices, the ones in their business professional
clothes in patriotic power colors, their faces swollen with anger and hatred
and sweat, tell

you

gaslight

you

criticize

you

hurt

you

prevent

you

legislate

you

denigrate

you

fail to protect

you

because they see that you,

a woman,

have one role in this world, to keep the

hearth and home

where you grow and give birth to

babies

that those same hatred-stricken faces won't protect from

guns

when those babies are old enough to go to

school

and won't fund programs to feed those babies when they're

hungry

because they say it is a moral flaw in your character that you can't

support

the children and the family that they

forced

us into having, regardless of whether a woman wants to have a family because it's not

safe

it's not

affordable—

it's not what she wants.

It's not natural to want anything else, they say, the ones in the patriotic business wear. Hence, that is why we are the

problem.

What they fail to realize is that this is all connected, that the control of one group is the control of everyone that is not a direct beneficiary of power. Mass shootings in schools, the climate crisis, bombing starving children, and women's rights are all pieces

of the same

puzzle

but control only works if those doing the controlling prevent everyone else
from seeing the bigger

picture

to keep us in the place they believe we should be in—the only place they
think we deserve:

less than.

⁂

⁂

⁂

Regardless of whether a woman wants to have children, having this disease
is a fellowship no one wishes to be a part of, myself included. Hormones are
out of balance, hair grows where other people say it shouldn't, and suddenly
my plans for life are disrupted by a body that simply says *maybe I can, but
maybe I can't*. It's not just my body, though. It's my brain that is increasingly
riddled with anxiety, a secondary condition sometimes associated with
PCOS, aggravated by living in a world where the body that carries that brain
around is constantly under attack. The bombardment comes from so many
sides that it's not possible to anticipate them all. I turn on the news each
morning while I eat breakfast, only to learn that another state has passed
increasingly ludicrous legislation not based on science but on one religion.
In my mind, I keep a picture of a map of the United States with more and
more states colored in dark, nighttime consuming everything between its
borders, knowing that it is not safe for me there. These are the places where
hopes, dreams, and the reality of accomplishing those hopes and dreams—of

having a family, of becoming a mother and having access to appropriate and necessary health care—cannot coexist.

The bombardment doesn't stop there. The news keeps coming, of war and genocide, of stagnant legislatures arguing over who is in charge of what, of wars and political threats to so many people's ability to just

exist

that are also nearly impossible to untangle myself from because of how our world works. There is no way to be proactive, only reactive, because when they take your

rights

one by one by one, it is difficult to be one step ahead when the rules of the game keep changing. First they came for

Planned Parenthood

and then they came for

Roe v. Wade

and then

IVF

and soon they could come for

contraception.

They call health care

murder

and say they're

protecting the innocent

while not caring about the

mothers.

All the while, the screaming faces in patriotic business wear disregard doctors, science, the research their government funds, or any sense of nuance that serves to break down the barriers of their rigid ideas of what a person a country a world should be. No one can know more understand more be more than they do and are. They do not care that abortion as a form of health care does more than end a pregnancy, that the issue is more complex. They forget about women like me who want to be

mothers

but live with illnesses and medical conditions that make motherhood

difficult

and who run higher risks of

miscarriage

that a woman's body may not be able to

release

on its own. I wonder how many of them understand that the procedure a woman has to undergo when her body won't release a miscarriage on its own is considered a form of abortion that is

medically necessary

to prevent

harm.

Five times greater

is the statistic that stares me in the face about my chances of having a miscarriage, if I am even able to conceive. At my age, the infamous biological clock is ticking, but now, it exists alongside a political one that counts down to an inevitable moment if we, collectively, do not change

our mindset

our laws

our politics

our society

and stop seeing women as less than, as objects to keep home, hearth, and health of others—but not our own. Tools, devices, means to ends that others want accomplished but aren't "their job," as if gender roles are as natural as respiration. They aren't.

A friend once asked me if the world wouldn't be like this if a certain dystopian book people like to reference in the fight for women's rights, reproductive and all the other ones, had never been published and given people ideas. The reality is that the book didn't give anyone any ideas—for many women, the world has always been this way.

I just want to be seen as a whole person, not a means to an end, an object, a mechanism, a conduit for the survival of a species, a way to help carry on a last name that wasn't originally mine to begin with.

☀

☀

What could be next?

I walk through a world that I try to make a better place for someone, even if that is one small step at a time that hardly anyone notices. I think about the world that I want to someday hand off to my children, a world in which I have taught them to revel in the wonder that is being alive and surrounded by an untold number of possibilities. The reality of those dreams, though, is that this is a world that is unkind at minimum to women and, at maximum, seeks to reduce women to nothing. The irony is that I may not survive bringing those children into this world, all because of courts and legislatures prioritizing their rights over those who have the most to lose. I wonder what the women who have come before me think, knowing that the women they worked so hard to change the world for live in a time where a

zip code

can be both a way of directing your mail and a

death sentence.

Those who are the most vulnerable are always the ones who are forced into the shadows, left to exist in places that are out of sight, out of mind for those who don't want to see us. Having PCOS is a pittance in the face of the atrocities that we collectively have committed against many marginalized communities. I can't help but wonder what will happen next. I watch the news with weary bones, constantly bracing myself for the next attack, wondering just how much longer this will last until enough someones have spoken up or those in power have achieved what they set out to do. How much longer before they come for the pills sitting in the green plastic case on the counter in my bathroom, the ones that radically changed my ability to exist because they regulated my hormones. How much longer before they take that away? How much longer before I am reduced to nothing more than a means to an end, a vessel, an object, instead of being fully seen and protected as a

person.

The future of our humanity—regardless of gender—hangs in the balance of just how far we allow those in power to go. There are days where the thought of speaking up again drains any ounce of energy from me; another generic email reply, another screen congratulating me on successfully submitting my concerns, or another dead-end phone number all sound like interactions I am increasingly less emotionally capable of. Instead, those are the days where I want to scream, to kick and throw things, to release the rage that I continually bury deep deep deep in my soul because I am not supposed to be

angry

because I am a

woman.

On other days, though, I do the emailing and submitting and calling because I remind myself

I have no choice

if

I still want to have a choice

in how I exist.

During those bouts of anger, I think back to the woman confined to the small box of her interview and the criticism she faced. What are her hopes and dreams? Does she just want someone to love her for who she is, including what she can't control? Does she someday hope to have children of her own? Or does she want to reach across her bed in the middle of the night and touch someone who loves and cares about her instead of cold sheets left unwrinkled? I wonder about her and how she feels as she moves through a world that increasingly pushes her to the side, too. It's just a matter of how geography, religion, and money factor into the equation as to how forcefully and how far she is pushed to the side because she is a woman with facial hair.

Imagining a different world is so difficult when the current one we live in burn burn burns in a way that threatens our existence. It's not just the trees or the ice caps or the air that is burning. It is also the hate that refuses to center

women

and

anyone who exists at the margins

because that would mean those too firmly stuck in their ways will have to change their mind about what makes a person a

person.

The exhaustion of existing courses through my veins with each heartbeat, permeating the marrow of my cells. There are mornings where the alarm clock rings, church bells echoing their greeting within the walls of my bedroom with the windows facing the rising sun, and I just want to stay in bed. I wonder what the point in trying is, that this world is one in which Civil War-era laws that predate a state's statehood can be enforced for the purpose of restricting access to health care, where the structural inequities in our health care system are so deeply entrenched that

Black women

die in childbirth at a rate 2.6 times white and Hispanic women, where children

are

starving

and

dying

because we live in a country that would rather fund

bombs

and

war

and

mass destruction

than

research

and

education

and

health care for all.

Waking up each day to the news of more and more steps backward makes it more difficult. Sometimes I wonder if waking up and just not leaving my bed will mean I exist far enough off the radar of those at the top of the food chain that they will leave me alone. Will let me live the life I want to live, a life where I am a good person who is seen as full, whole, and worthy. Will let me exist as a person who matters and is protected and has what I need without having to continuously break my mind, body, and spirit to have basic necessities. If the goal is to make so many people

not exist

then why try to

exist

at all? And when people ask

why

others haven't commented on genocide or

why

others haven't spoken up on the latest round of hate- and intolerance-based legislation or

why

others aren't doing more or

why

others aren't marching or

why

others aren't protesting or demonstrating or threatening to burn it all to the ground, I want to remind them of the weariness that comes with just getting out of bed in the morning, of living in a world that is being rebuilt to be for you only if you will

submit

and

comply

with standards and expectations that you may or may not be able to meet through no fault or choice of your own.

But what do we know? We just live in these bodies, the ones whose biology others want to obsess over in ways that place

politics over protection,
reproduction over rights,
anatomy over acceptance.

It's not even the science of the matter, because after several long years of living in a world where we kind of sort of maybe possibly acknowledge how the world is fundamentally less safe, we're still denying the

science

that saves lives. We as women—all women—can't know our own bodies better than politicians, than preachers, than our neighbors who vote the checkbox next to the candidates whose names will later crawl across the bottom of the screen in red as election results roll in like tidal waves.

I wonder what the woman in the Twitter interview box would have said to me if my phone's settings had been anything but what they were. The reality of the matter is that it doesn't matter what she would or wouldn't have said—because who would be listening? Who would care? I often wonder who out there does care, as the exhaustion settles in like the thick morning fog in the moments before dawn, gathering along the ground to make reality less clear. As the days go by, I fear the people who do care are the ones who are less and less capable of doing something about it. With each breaking news moment about how a small group of people have changed life for everyone in a large way, it is increasingly more difficult to say something, anything, without those at the top coming for whatever they can get to keep people quiet. But what do we know, those who must live this existence?

But do they—

the politicians
the religious leaders
the media
the voters who swear they will only ever vote red
the ones who believe the extremes
the ones who insist they're never heard but are listened to the most
the ones who are not scientists and yet insist they know what is and
isn't natural—

what will you do now, now that your friends, your mothers sisters daughters—everyone you know, not just women—are in danger, too?

Field Notes on What Adorns Us

A Case Study

PURPOSE: to examine approaches to and attitudes toward bodily adornment, how people adorn their bodies and why, and personal reasons for body modification.

Introduction

This study focuses on a single subject. [SUBJECT] is a cis-gendered woman in her midthirties. [SUBJECT] is a writer who has chosen to remain anonymous. She is described as around average height, heavyset, with brown hair, blue eyes, and glasses. [SUBJECT] has been diagnosed with polycystic ovarian syndrome (PCOS), which impacts how [SUBJECT] views her body. She has admitted to having at least one instance of adornment in two of the three categories examined in this study. She has considered acquiring adornments in the third category. These categories include piercings, scars, and tattoos.

[SUBJECT] is currently writing about femininity and the body. This study will make connections between [SUBJECT]'s experiences with and attitudes toward adornment as well as her creative interests. Additionally, this study will examine scholarly views on what I have termed as adornment but is more widely known as body modification.

Body modification is of particular interest to this researcher. This researcher has multiple roles in this case study, as this researcher is also [SUBJECT], the person whose experiences support this study. This researcher has an interest in other people's body modifications, especially tattoos. Additionally, this researcher is trying to connect personal and academic research in a way that situates [SUBJECT]'s experiences within a greater context.

Background

Scholarship has not always been friendly to the idea of body modification. Poet and therapist Kathleen Del Mar Miller cites scholars of body modification and somatechnics who have labeled the act of body modification as a hostile act directed at oneself out of hate or spite. Del Mar Miller references Nikki Sullivan, a scholar of body modification and somatechnics, as describing bodily adornment as extra-analytic; in other words, modifications to the body's flesh can be seen and commented on but are not available for analytic inquiry. In this case, body modification is an aesthetic trend to be viewed as either splendorous or monstrous, where meaning is over inscribed or nonexistent. In this line of thinking, tattoos and body piercings are compared to hairstyles or cuts of pants, in which their cultural relevance and value is more about being pleasing to the eye than anything else.

British independent scholar Kay Inckles cites psychiatry and criminology as fields that also view body piercing, tattooing, and scarring as a pathology. In this theory, if a person in a dualistic society, such as Western societies, has piercings, tattoos, or scars, then there must be a pathology behind those modifications because such behavior deviates from Western societal expectations and norms regarding how a body looks and acts. In the past, these adornments of the body and other forms of body modification have often been associated, at least in Western thought, with primitivism or with countercultures. This is a contentious association when looking at how "primitive" and "pathology" have been defined and those definitions' relationships to normativity.

These conclusions, however, are not representative of all fields of academic study. Anthropological research provides several perspectives on body modification in cultures around the globe that counter previously mentioned ideas about body modification. Scholar M. C. Taylor, who studies religious philosophy, argues that the cultural renaissance of tattooing in the 1980s was more than just a passing and trivial fad but instead makes the case that the wider acceptance of tattooing is a significant change due to the power involved with the materiality of the body. In a world where more and more bodies are increasingly virtual, Taylor argues that body modification worked to undo the dematerialization of the human body by making the human body matter.

On the other hand, a common theme among those who have studied body modification is its relationship to memory. Marks on the body's surface become a symbolic second skin that is meant to cover and protect the physical skin of the body. This protection symbolizes the rebirth of an individual who is more empowered to live as an authentic self. This is because, as psychologist Suzanne B. Phillips writes in *Psychology Today*, tattoos and tattooing in particular offer six qualities associated with recovering from trauma. Phillips cites multiple instances in which survivors of trauma have used tattooing to create this symbolic second skin, including women tattooing over mastectomy scars, military veterans commemorating their service to their country, parents honoring children who died, or people working through their part in larger cultural traumas.

Piercings

When asked about her piercings, [SUBJECT] disclosed the following list: first ear lobe piercings at age seven done at the Claire's in the mall, second ear lobe piercings done at age thirteen at the same Claire's in the same mall, helix piercing along the back curve of her left ear at age eighteen at the same Claire's in the same mall, navel at age eighteen when her friend also had an appointment for this piercing, the first nose piercing the same week as her nineteenth birthday at a studio on a state route out of the town where she went to college, the repiercing of her nose at twenty-nine shortly before her PCOS diagnosis and applying for PhD programs, and both daith piercings shortly after turning thirty-one in a partial attempt to alleviate migraines and in part "just for the hell of it."

[SUBJECT] has had few problems with her piercings, except for the first nose piercing, which she was afraid to show her parents because of her dad's views that people with facial piercings are punks with faces like Swiss cheese. This meant [SUBJECT] took her nose ring out when she went home for one weekend a month to work so she could keep her summer job at McDonald's, which at that time required that employees remove all their facial piercings or cover them up. When home for spring break, she lost her nose ring in the carpet of her childhood bedroom and was without a replacement for a week. By the time [SUBJECT] got back to campus, her nose piercing had grown shut enough that she was not able to put new jewelry in the piercing. [SUBJECT]'s body and its acceptance of body piercings means that she has no scars or disfiguration from the rejection of piercings or jewelry.

[SUBJECT] admits that the second ear lobe piercing on her right ear was slightly botched, sometimes making it difficult to insert jewelry. She wishes she had known that getting pierced with a piercing gun at the mall is considered a blunt-force trauma injury because of the piercing gun's mechanics. Obviously, this is not a safe way to pierce anything, and [SUBJECT] now knows better. "I can see the draw to getting your ears pierced at the mall, though," [SUBJECT] notes:

> It's safe getting your ears pierced at the mall because it is comfortable for a lot of people. Tattoo shops have a certain reputation around them for a lot of people, even though more and more people have tattoos and piercings that aren't in their ears. But getting your ears pierced at the mall is also a kind of performance. The piercing station is usually right by the door or, worse yet, one of those kiosks on the concourse. Everyone can see what you're doing. Everyone can also hear you screaming if you aren't prepared for what's about to happen, too. It says something about you and your parents but also tries to lessen the significance of what is happening. It's a way of saying, "Hey, this child or adult is about to do something traumatizing to their body because it's also pretty, but that's okay—you can buy stuff or go get a pretzel in the food court after you're done!"

[SUBJECT] now only gets piercings done by professionals who know what they're doing. "It's just safer that way," she says, remembering how her cartilage crunched when the woman at the mall used a piercing gun on her helix.

[SUBJECT] notes that she often "feels the itch" for a new piercing to mark the start or end of a period in her life. [SUBJECT] says that the ear lobe piercings are an exception that she asked for as a child because she wanted to be like her mom, which [SUBJECT] says that, as an adult, she sees as an early attempt at modeling femininity:

> I mean, all the women in my family had their ears pierced. Well, almost all of them, I think. But when you're used to seeing women with shiny things in their ears and you don't have any, I think it's a natural impulse to want piercings, too. That goes for both sets of my ear lobe piercings—when I saw that my mom

could wear *two* pairs of earrings at the same time, I wondered, well, why couldn't I do that, too?

The second attempt at piercing her nose and her daith piercings marked slightly different occasions. "Honestly, I missed my nose piercing," [SUBJECT] said. "I was kind of attached to it. Sometimes, though, I just feel that I need a change. With my daith piercings, I had them done a couple of months after a serious breakup and I was in my last semester of taking classes as a student—like, last semester *ever*—and it felt like a lot in my life was drastically shifting at that time."

In the future, [SUBJECT] is considering a forward helix piercing on her right ear since she was told her tragus, the small point of cartilage that hides the opening to the ear canal, is not big enough to survive a piercing. The forward helix, or a piercing of the outer rim of the ear, is said to be a rather painful piercing, which so far is why [SUBJECT] has not followed through with her plan—yet.

Scars

[SUBJECT] admits to having a variety of scars and marks with varying degrees of visibility and intent. The earliest one [SUBJECT] remembers recognizing is on her left forearm, about two inches below her elbow. [SUBJECT] maintains that she was stung by a bee as a child, and the sting left behind a dark spot about a third of the size of a quarter. [SUBJECT] says her mother claims that the spot has always been there, leaving [SUBJECT] to wonder if it is a scar or a birthmark and if classification really matters at all.

Over the course of our interview, [SUBJECT] revealed an accidental scar less visible than the mark on her arm. This scar is a result of spilling a large amount of boiling pasta water on her stomach while making dinner for Mother's Day when she was twenty-seven. "I was about to pour the pasta into the strainer I had in the sink," [SUBJECT] said, "and I thought I heard someone say my name. I was startled and the pasta water went all over my stomach. I've burned myself on accident a lot, but this one hurt the worst." Initially, [SUBJECT] said that the wound from the pasta water incident hurt so bad and blistered so much of her stomach that she could barely stand to feel clothes rubbing against the injury. As the blistering subsided and the scar rose shiny and new to the surface, [SUBJECT] claims that it might have been the funniest-looking scar she has had because it looked like a T. Rex chasing bubbles. Since then, the scar has faded so much that it is barely visible.

Additional scars include a red splotch on [SUBJECT]'s right shoulder from a benign cyst, random freckles, spots of discoloration from acne, picked-at bug bites from childhood, and stretch marks on [SUBJECT]'s stomach. [SUBJECT] remarks that her stretch marks have a slightly holographic quality to them, which she suspects is a result of major shifts in her body shape over time: puberty; significant weight gain in her preteen and early teenage years that resulted in visits to a dietician and a prescription for Metformin, a drug meant to control blood sugar, that her pediatrician kept increasing because [SUBJECT] wasn't losing weight fast enough; and the three years [SUBJECT] put her education and most of her career aspirations on hold after college to help care for her maternal grandmother, who had dementia and was increasingly limited in her mobility on top of [SUBJECT] needing to figure out what she wanted to do with her life. [SUBJECT] reveals that her reaction to the second major shift in body shape also involved periods of drastically reducing the number of calories she consumed, which was self-inflicted, and that the third major shift was counteracted not only by the onset of the fitness tracker craze but also due to a proper diagnosis and medication.

When I asked how she felt about these scars, [SUBJECT] remarked that she oscillates between indifference and feeling that her stretch marks sometimes make her feel monstrous. This researcher hypothesizes that this has a direct relationship not only to body image but to a belated diagnosis of her PCOS and the impact that violent patriarchy has on a woman. Additionally, this researcher thinks that [SUBJECT]'s frustration and anger over repeated misunderstandings and blame directed at her adds to how [SUBJECT] thinks about her stretch marks. [SUBJECT] has heard plenty of times that she isn't trying hard enough. [SUBJECT] has tried, sometimes trying too hard in not the best of ways.

Although [SUBJECT] does not disclose details here, she mentions scars that are no longer or never were visible. Two of these scars were, [SUBJECT] admits, on her abdomen at the bottom of her ribcage from a particularly dark period in her teenage years. Others are mental or emotional scars. When asked for further information, [SUBJECT] says that these scars tend to fall into several different categories: disappointment, betrayal, repeated misunderstandings, varying forms of violence, and another that [SUBJECT] says, even with her specialized knowledge of words and language, is difficult to explain. To quote [SUBJECT], "Frustration isn't strong enough of a word, but I'm not sure anger is the right word either. It's a mixture of both, I think. What makes it hard to think about is, somewhere along the way, ambivalence got tangled up in there, too. Probably as a defense mechanism, to be honest. If I don't feel it, then it can't keep hurting me—right?" [SUBJECT] acknowledges that this is not the most effective coping mechanism nor does suppressing what bothers her prevent it from hurting her.

Tattoos

Surprisingly, [SUBJECT] revealed during her interviews that she does not have tattoos. She is intrigued by them and appreciates other people's tattoos, but her indecisiveness about what she would want to be marked on her body for the rest of her life has prevented her from getting one.

[SUBJECT] has a Pinterest board of potential tattoo ideas, most of which consist of flowers (particularly cherry blossoms), elephants with their trunks raised, lotus flowers, references to books or poetry, or the Latin phrase *alis volat propriis*. [SUBJECT] appears drawn to tattoos of delicate flowers, as this Pinterest board also has examples of tattoos of wildflowers, daisies, and dandelions gone to seed. "I just like flowers," [SUBJECT] commented. "There's always a simplicity in how beautiful they are, and there's something about flowers that are very natural—they don't have to try to be flowers or perform flower-ness."

In addition to flowers, [SUBJECT] has saved tattoos of elephants with trunks held high. [SUBJECT] explained that her maternal grandmother, who lived next door until she died of dementia and pneumonia when [SUBJECT] was twenty-five, collected elephants with trunks up in the air. "They're supposed to be good luck," [SUBJECT] said.

In an ideal world, [SUBJECT] says, if money, pain, and time weren't issues, she would get a tattoo of a whole swath of cherry blossoms, spreading from one hip across her back to the opposite shoulder blade and ribs. [SUBJECT] has the details planned out. Shades of pink with accents of cerulean and bright green on soft brown branches. The style would be soft, somewhere between a traditionally outlined tattoo and the watercolor style. When asked about the likelihood of getting such a tattoo, [SUBJECT] simply shrugged. "I don't know," she said. "Maybe someday."

Conclusion

Despite arguments from those, including [SUBJECT], who view adornment as both a method of expression and reclamation, [SUBJECT] feels that the threat of violence, something that has been documented, causes her to hesitate before adorning her body:

> I feel like—well, there isn't really a feeling, it's basically a fact—that there are ways in which my body has already been marked in very public ways. The fact that I'm a woman with this disease that changed both my outward appearance and how my body functions is one way. My body visibly takes up space, more space than it "should" take up. And how society has developed ways to make you feel like something is wrong with you because you couldn't control yourself, even if there wasn't anything that you could control, is aggressive and ugly and causes me to think a lot about what control I have over the ways my body is marked. In some ways, the less visible I feel my body is, the safer I can be because I'm not drawing attention to myself. I won't be asked questions. I won't have to interpret what that stare is supposed to mean. I won't have to analyze a doctor's tone of voice or facial expression. I can just go about my life in the body I have.

Of particular interest to this researcher is how [SUBJECT] makes the connection between adornment and memory. [SUBJECT] said:

> Yeah, I think that's why I keep pushing the idea of getting a tattoo into the future. There are definitely things I want to commemorate, like the elephant tattoo for my grandma, but I also think . . . there's that frustration/anger/ambivalence piece to it, too. That I've gotten so good at not only suppressing things that have happened to me that I can't name those emotions anymore so I don't know what I would attempt to reclaim.

When asked if piercings differ from tattoos, [SUBJECT] talks about permanence: "With a piercing, I always have the opportunity to change my mind," [SUBJECT] said. "If I don't like it or feel that it isn't 'me' anymore, I can take the jewelry out and let it grow closed. I've never done that on purpose, but the allure of having that option is there. Of course, there may be a scar and scar tissue under the skin, but it's a lot easier to get rid of a piercing than it is a tattoo." [SUBJECT] had to think when asked if these attitudes are related to memory and the changes her body has gone through. "Maybe they are related," [SUBJECT] said. "Maybe it's because if I change the ways I think about what I've gone through and how I name those feelings, then the option to change the ways I've adorned myself are still there. But a tattoo—that's there forever. I'm not sure if I'm ready for . . . I'm not sure if I'm at a point where I can do that yet."

A point of curiosity, and a bigger question that this case study aimed to examine, was how all of this relates to ideas of femininity and identity. "I think it causes me to sometimes overthink how my body appears in public—from what I'm wearing to what is marked on my skin—and how other people think they understand me as a person based on my appearance," said [SUBJECT]. "It's exhausting, but when I have a day where I feel like I don't really give a care, I feel extra visible. As in, I feel more visible because I don't care, and my lack of care is seen as an invitation for comment, which then makes me think about what that stare means or what that person is saying when they ask me a question. So I have these options in front of me where I can be exhausted and somewhat safe or I can be somewhat carefree and feel overly visible.

"But really, I think the direction we're headed collectively is toward acceptance of adorned women, of women who have piercings and tattoos and scars. It's not because our ideas of what 'normal' femininity is have drastically changed but because more women are willing to express themselves through what is on their skin."

[SUBJECT] has ideas for future study on body adornment. "I read an article that talked about women and scars and popular culture, and the line that really stood out to me talked about culture finding beauty in stories that have left a mark on us. That line hit a nerve and makes a lot of sense, even if we can't quite put those stories into words." In response to the question of whether [SUBJECT] will ever find the words to put her stories together in a way that adorns her, [SUBJECT]'s response was rather straightforward.

"Someday."

Sifting the Feminine Bones

Freytag's Pyramid is an ultimate form of deception.

Even if a person is not a writer, they likely know what Freytag's Pyramid is without the formal name. As I call it when I teach the shape to my students, it's "the funny-looking triangle" designed by its namesake German novelist in the 1800s to describe the shape of certain stories. Over the years, it has become the most recognizable shape of a story, regardless of genre or culture. One might even call it the bully of story shapes, intimidating all others out of sight and out of mind.

There is more than one shape writers use to tell stories. The idea that this is *the* shape of a story, this oddly shaped triangle, leaves out so many other shapes, so many other stories. It forces a limited view on what a story can do, what it can be. That limiting force pushes stories into a corner where the number of possibilities shrink. The number of ways we think about ourselves shrinks, too. The whole world shrinks.

Stories do not all have the same shape, just as not all bodies have the same shape. The idea of a universal shape of stories or bodies does not work for everyone. Nor should it work for everyone.

CHAPTER 1: Exposition, aka The Introduction

I sometimes marvel at how smooth the introduction, the exposition, is shown to be in drawings of the shapes of stories. I guess it's a collective sense of idealism that causes us to want that introduction to be smooth, to have something that isn't necessarily perfect, but is as close to perfect as possible.

When I think of the story of my body, the exposition part of the story is not flat and smooth. If anything, I think of this part of the story shaped like two separate threads, intertwining with one another like a ribbon or the double helix of a person's DNA.

Stories are a part of who I am. Instead of putting headphones on her belly and playing classical music for me before I was born, my mom read me stories. I was surrounded by stories, whether those found in books or ones told to me by other family members. As a child, I ran around the open spaces of my rural backyard and my mother's family farm as if boundaries did not exist, as if I lived in the stories told to me and I was simply a whirlwind, a wisp of a spirit on its next adventure. When you're small and the space around you seems so vast, so unending, the possibility for new stories is infinite, even if I didn't recognize where one story ended and another began.

Not only have stories always been a part of who I am, but so has my body. I've watched the family videos and looked at the photo albums, and in them, I appear to be an average child. Not too short, not too tall. Not too thin, but not chubby either. I wonder if there was an inkling that something could go wrong and, if so, when would the catalyst be activated. If I think of the shape of this moment, the introduction, as two strands twisted together, points of contact or intersection between storytelling and my body are moments where something happened. Maybe not *the* catalyst, but small reactions along the way that intertwined my body and storytelling to the point where the two have merged into almost, but not quite, one.

Maybe those points of contact between storytelling and my body were, in retrospect, moments of foreshadowing. Just as a writer creates hints and forecasts on a page, maybe there was something indicating what was about to happen, creating tension but also warning me that girlhood is something different from womanhood. In girlhood, there were still warnings—the criticisms of my body starting at such a young age—that set off alarms I was unable to hear. Those alarms weren't just about me, but also how the meaning of womanhood would drastically change in the years to come.

Warning, something should have told me—*you're approaching a moment at which, whether you like it or not, you can't go back.*

CHAPTER 2: The Inciting Incident

Is there only one inciting incident in a story?

After writing the introduction, I think of revisions. I wonder if I have a place in the introduction of my story and how it changes what the inciting incident is. I can think of several, but each one asks to follow a different introduction. The onset of puberty is one of them and the way my body struggled to work the way it was supposed to at this point in my life; I "bloomed early," a phrase meant more to signal politeness than anything else. The moment I realized that my body wasn't acting in the same ways as my friends at our age. The look on my pediatrician's face when she read over my charts. Any number of ways I noticed I was different.

Instead of a single point where the trajectory changes, this scenario looks like multiple threads that occasionally come together, only to result in an explosion that changes the course of the story. The pyramid is no longer straightforward in its neat and clean lines but instead looks like a mess before the story starts. The pyramid was never as neat and clean as it appeared to be.

I wonder if another inciting incident in the story of my body is the moment of my birth, that coming into this world as a living, breathing being was the moment that changed the trajectory of a story I didn't know I was a part of. Maybe by virtue of being born, I've changed the narrative, but making that statement makes me feel uncomfortable. But it gives my story a fixed point in history—a date, a time, a place, and even the peculiarity of an ice storm and the coldest day of the winter that year. Here, the introduction would be something that looked more like a lineage. Whether it's a family lineage or a lineage of women of which I am a tiny part, there are threads of stories that all somehow lead to one inciting incident early in the morning on a cold winter's day.

In another draft, I lose track of just what the inciting incident could be. The story of my body is just another thin thread in a greater story of what it means to be a woman. I wonder if the inciting incident was an agreement between genes that decided I was going to be born with a certain body, unlocking a particular world I was to be a part of and figure out. Maybe it is a combination of two threads, one where femininity is both threatened and threatening. That story is an example of what patriarchy does when a woman's body does not fit the narrative, does not behave in the way that it is supposed to so all the structures continue functioning. This is the point where the inciting incident has the potential to bring the whole structure of the story tumbling to the ground, creating something new out of the kicked up dust.

CHAPTER 3: Rising Action

The rising action is, in my opinion, one of the most difficult parts of a story to write. A writer must know a lot of details about their story before sitting down to write to make the rising action of a story do the work that it needs to do. A careful choreography happens here. A writer can't reveal too many details too early or hold onto them for too long. A writer can keep throwing plot twists and turns at their characters. They can use breaks and space to create tension as the rising action continues to build. At some point, a writer must reveal what is at stake for the person at the center of the story. Without this choreography, the rest of the story unravels.

In the story of my body, the rising action splits into multiple lanes, like the widening of a highway as it approaches the crest of a hill.

One lane is the story of my body developing and discovering what it can do. Along the way, there are several moments when a doctor, someone—anyone—should have noticed that something wasn't right. There were partial realizations, but no one put together all the pieces to realize that not everything that was medically "wrong" with my body was entirely my fault. No one seemed to put the causes and effects together in the correct order until, in some ways, it was too late. I had already formed an understanding of my body, what it does, and what I hoped it would do in the future. The rising action here diffuses at its height, the moment when the story turns, the moment I knew my plans for life may not be as easily realized as I previously thought. After all, at the same time I was learning about desire and femininity, I was told that my body is not acceptable and that I needed to change it.

Even though I hadn't put a name to my experiences, it was also in the rising action of my story that I learned that there is a link between desire and violence, that one can incite the other, that the two can become entangled in ways that feel damning and contradictory. At times, it did. I turned that violence on myself not knowing the full extent of what was happening under my skin. I don't know how this story would have changed if I had known the full extent of what I went through. Maybe it would have changed. Maybe it wouldn't have. Maybe there are parts of this story that wouldn't exist had someone put the pieces together sooner.

I wonder if it's possible that, if someone had been a little less certain somewhere along this slope of rising action, then maybe the rest of my story would have been different.

Another lane in the rising action of the story of my body is learning that the world is not always a safe place for women, even though it is safer for me than it is for many women. The places and people that I thought were safe and always would be safe might be the places where the violence creeps in, seeps in at the edges I thought were sealed against the outside world. The communities and structures meant to protect me, such as the government but also loved ones, places of work, and places of play—slowly became the very people and places that I could no longer trust in their entirety. In this part of the rising action, there are a series of lessons strung together that, had I heard the warning bells as a child, would have made more sense. Maybe the price of femininity would have made more sense, that even though there is power to be had and held as a woman, there are also prices to pay as a particular kind of woman, one whose story takes a different shape.

CHAPTER 4: Climax

No matter what the path toward the climax is, this is the moment where all the threads coalesce into one moment that I can say with certainty changed the narrative—or so I thought.

There were reasons beyond medicine for my experiences. When one's femininity does not fall in line with what is expected, the potential for both being seen as a threat and to be on the receiving end of violence increases greatly. A woman's body not being able to act and do some of the things that society and culture has constructed as inherently female poses a risk. After all, what happens if a multitude of femininities were to exist? What happens if a woman, if a person, if I, were able to define femininity on my own terms and society and culture were okay with it?

What would happen if I were allowed to grieve a change in that understanding without the baggage of knowing change meant there were other ways in which violence could come at me?

What would happen if I could have just grieved a change in how I understood my body without having to think about what a life of consequences of this disease would look like?

That is a question that, as the days go on and the rights of women are continually eroded, I cannot answer. In looking back through the generations, my mom had more rights than I do at the age I am at now. I had more rights at five years old—the age I was when my mom was the same age I am now as I sit here and write this—than I do as an adult. I can't find a way to frame or think about consequences when the trigger for those consequences gets more and more sensitive, when I am more and more likely to suffer the consequences while committing an action with the best of intentions. The only motive I have for some kind of moral failure is that my ideologies and my body, through no choice of my own, do not align with someone else's expectations for the story my body is supposed to play a part in.

Maybe the structure would come tumbling down.

But it won't. *Fit in. Follow the narrative,* they say. *If your story doesn't fit the pyramid, we will bury you under it.*

CHAPTER 5: Falling Action

The slope toward resolution involves a lot of learning, unlearning, and resisting.

I've had to learn a lot about myself. I've had to evaluate not only the ways I think about my body but the ways I've been told that my body was wrong or not right over the course of a lifetime. I still have decades of learning to rethink and reimagine. The work of editing and revising one's story is difficult and draining, especially when the story is being revised on one end while being written on the other.

Sometimes, the falling action, the slide into resolution, includes twists and turns. The downward slope toward resolution isn't as sleek as it looks. There are bumps, and there are more turning points. Sometimes, there are craters to climb out of.

CHAPTER 6: The Resolution, The Denouement, or "The Unraveling of the Knot"

I don't know what the resolution to this story is.

I could argue that the resolution is some form of acceptance, that I have come to terms with the fact that I have this disease. Those changes also make me rethink what it means to be in a body that I and others have decided is a woman's body. This resolution doesn't fit, though, because I haven't found a form of absolute acceptance. Acceptance, in this case, feels like resignation, that I know I have a condition where x is happening and could potentially cause a whole bunch of y-associated health problems as I continue with my life. Acceptance feels like shrugging my shoulders and giving in. Resignation feels like giving up any hope that I might be able to do something about my body. Both acceptance and resignation feel much too passive for the person I am, as if they're different forms of standing aside and letting whatever happens to my body happen.

Having my disease "under control," as doctors would say, is another resolution for this story. I have learned how to live with my PCOS, and therefore, my story and my body have returned to status-quo-sub-prime, a slightly varied yet forever different version of who I was. This doesn't feel like a resolution either because, though my disease is under control, I don't always feel like I am in control of my disease. The random onsets of pain, the unexplained shifts in weight, the changes in my diet because of a newly discovered food allergy that also amplifies the effects of my hormonal imbalance. The fact that my health will always be something that puts me at risk for things far more worrisome and scarier—not just medical conditions but the legislating of the moral character of my body to do what others want it to do in the way they want it done—does not feel like control, regardless of what preposition someone decides to put in front of the key word.

Control.

In or under?

This feels like another false resolution, a knot not quite unraveled because there are still pages and pages left to go.

I could argue that the resolution to the story of my body only arrives in death but that is terrifying. The anxiety wakes in my chest, muscles tighten, my breath quickens and comes in shallow gulps for air. This is something I have thought about, a delve into what the future looks like that makes my pulse race easier than almost anything. PCOS is not fatal. There are enough associated health conditions that stem from the effects of PCOS that can end my life to cause a disconnect between my self and my body—fear of what could happen, when it could happen, and whether it will be this or that or something completely different that will be the cause of my stilled heart, relaxed lungs, silenced mind.

I try not to think too much because to think about what could happen causes an existential terror that freezes me in place, allowing a dread to settle into my bones that takes days to shake off.

It could be a heart attack or heart disease.

It could be complications from diabetes, something I spent the first twenty-five years of my life watching my maternal grandmother fight until something else ended her life.

It could be a stroke.

It could be cancer.

It could be complications from a miscarriage, something I am five times more likely to experience and increasingly have less access to the needed medical care to address.

It could be something else entirely.

The writer in me is both frustrated and terrified that so much of the resolution to the story of my body is unknown. This twisted shape of Freytag's Pyramid does not fit the story I am trying to convey, and none of the options available work the way I want them to. Unfortunately, the shape of a story doesn't always look the way that a writer, or even a reader, wants it to look and act and be. Sometimes, the story itself is just too powerful to be able to control.

The story of my body is not the only thread that is headed toward resolution. I am reminded that there are forces beyond me at play here, and those stories are continually working toward a resolution that those forces do not want. Those stories are a threat to the ones society and culture have told us, all of us, about how the world works, about how people are supposed to be and move through a world those forces helped create. I am reminded that, in some ways, I will always be fighting against someone else's story of my body, one that says *that one over there, that one writing a different story—well, she just couldn't follow the directions. She didn't write a story that looks like it should.*

She was even given a picture.

Fit in. Follow the narrative, they say. *If your story doesn't fit the pyramid, we will bury you under it.*

Sometimes I wonder where the line is between not wanting to write that story and needing to write a different one.

There are times when that weight is too much. The grief comes back to the surface when I think about the moments when the criticisms hurled at me layer themselves on one another. The moments when I feel like the monster inside of me exists in a way that is too great. The moments when carrying the burden of telling a different story is too much to carry. I know I am not the only one, and the weight of that story is not as great as others, but there are still days when my story is too much.

There are times in those moments when I catch myself in a mirror. It might be the one in the bathroom in my apartment. It might be the rearview mirror in my car or another mirror entirely. The sight of my reflection causes me to stop. There are times when I stop and, dare I say it, admire my reflection. I see that the courage and strength I attribute to other women is in me, too, and despite knowing what I do about my body and what the future may hold, the story of my body has also made me strong enough to continue carrying that weight and to do something with it.

There are instances when my reflection catches me off guard. I don't breathe. My eyes start to sting. The weight becomes too much, and, if I am alone, I look away and cry.

I can only hold my breath for so long.

I feel myself, internally and externally, change shape. I feel the tears pooling at the corners of my eyes, threatening to spill over again and again. I can only hold in so much.

I exhale.

I inhale.

The story continues—it has no other choice if I want to do the same.

Brooke Champagne, *Nola Face: Memoirs of a Truth-Telling Latina in the Big Easy*

Maddie Norris, *The Wet Wound: An Elegy in Essays*

Cris Mazza, *The Decade of Letting Things Go: A Postmenopause Memoir*

Lydia Paar, *The Exit Is the Entrance: Essays on Escape*

Joe Bonomo, *Play This Book Loud: Noisy Essays*

Wes Jamison, *My Corpse Inside*

Ashley Anderson, *Sifting the Feminine: Essays on a Woman's Body*